Training Mules
and Donkeys

A Logical Approach to Longears

Equine Management
and
Donkey Training

by Meredith Hodges

"PEGASSES"

Printed in the United States of America

First Edition

Cover photo by Wayne Crownhart
Cover design by Ann Clarke
Text design and layout by Willman Productions and Vision Graphics
Editing by Eagle-Eye Indexing and Editing

ISBN 1-928624-16-2

DISCLAIMER

The information contained in this book will give the reader a broad perspective of training mules and donkeys. The intent of this book is to provide as much information as possible about training mules and donkeys so that individuals are able to make their own decisions regarding training activities and equipment to use.

While the training techniques offered in this book set high standards for safety, all equine activities inherently involve some risk. Meredith Hodges, Lucky Three Ranch, and Willman Productions are not liable for the injury or death of any individual participating in equine activities after reading this book or viewing any of the videotapes.

COPYRIGHT

Write to: MediaTech Productions c/o Maury Willman
      P.O. Box 272345
      Fort Collins, CO 80527
      970-224-5911   www.mediatechproductions.com

Customer Service and Orders:
      1-800-816-7566

Lucky Three Ranch, Inc.
Meredith Hodges
2457 South County Road 19
Loveland, CO 80537
970-663-0066 phone   970-663-0676 fax
LuckyThreeRanch.com   equineoutlet.com
Email: lucky3@willman.com

INTRODUCTION

This book is a collection of the information covered in Videotapes #8 through #10 in the videotape series, ***Training Mules and Donkeys: A Logical Approach to Longears***. This book and the companion videotapes are designed to help you understand mules and donkeys and learn how to handle and train them effectively. The book is divided into three parts, each of which corresponds to one of the three videotapes in the series. A workbook and field cards are also provided with each videotape to summarize and supplement the information presented on the videotape, so there is no need to take notes. (Videotapes #1 through #7 are summarized in the spiral bound book, *Training Without Resistance: From Foal to Advanced Levels*.)

If you would like more in-depth explanations about some of the methods and techniques, refer to the hardbound books, *Training Mules and Donkeys: A Logical Approach to Longears* and *Donkey Training*, both by Meredith Hodges.

We recommend that you approach Meredith's entire series of videotapes from the beginning, starting with Videotape #1 and advancing in sequence to the other tapes. All of the information is provided in a logical sequence and will be most meaningful if you view the videotapes in order. Whether you are re-training to correct problems or starting a mule who has never been trained, begin with Part 1 of Meredith's spiral bound workbook, *Training Without Resistance: From Foal to Advanced Levels*, and/or Videotape #1 to establish the proper foundation from which to build.

Created by renowned mule expert, Meredith Hodges, the videotapes feature simple, easy-to-follow lessons designed to teach you a variety of correct and effective training methods. The result will be a beautiful, well-mannered, well-trained, modern mule!

There are a total of ten tapes in Meredith's videotape training series:

Videotape #1:   Foal Training
Videotape #2:   Preparing for Performance: Ground Work
Videotape #3:   Preparing for Performance: Driving
Videotape #4:   Basic Foundation for Saddle
Videotape #5:   Intermediate Saddle Training
Videotape #6:   Advanced Saddle Training
Videotape #7:   Jumping
Videotape #8:   Management, Fitting, and Grooming
Videotape #9:   Donkey Training: Introduction and Basic Training
Videotape #10: Donkey Training: Saddle Training and Jumping

For details on how to order any of the materials in this series, refer to the last pages of this book.

ACKNOWLEDGMENTS

A quick disclaimer ("to cover our butts"): the following titles are not meant
to offend—but to induce a bit of laughter—enjoy!

"BIG ASS" PRODUCER	• Maury Willman (President/CEO of MediaTech Productions)
"ASS EXPERT & SMART ASS"	• Meredith Hodges (Author, trainer, expert in donkeys and mules. Owner of Lucky Three Ranch)
PRODUCTION COMPANY	• MediaTech Productions (Fort Collins, CO)
NARRATORS	• Rick Noffsinger (Combined Driving Instructor/Trainer, Loveland, CO) • David Hartley
ORIGINAL MUSIC BY	• Blake & the Super Donks 'Unbridled Love' 'Hoofin' It' 'Giddy-up' 'Lord of the Prance' 'Saddle Up Sally' 'Muck Bucket Blues' 'Slow Rye'
PRODUCTION STAFF	• Blake Miller of CSI Film and Video, Fort Collins, CO (Director of Photography & "Smart Ass") • Robbie Aukerman of CSI Film and Video (Art & Animation Director, "Ass-istant" to Photography) • Michelle McIntosh ("Ass-istant" to Ass Trainer) • Dena Hodges ("Lil' Smart Ass") • Jarah Komrs of MediaTech Productions ("Ass-istant" to Producer) • Tony Servin, Lucky Three Ranch (Best Boy or Ass Trainer's "Ass-ential") • Scott Collins ("Ass"-istant to Best Boy)
SCREEN WRITER	• Ann Clarke (Personal Promotion Specialist, Fort Collins, CO and "Screenwriter who's Ass-less")
GRAPHIC ARTIST	• Ann Clarke (Personal Promotion Specialist)
WORKBOOK & FIELD CARD WRITER	• Maury Willman (MediaTech Productions)
WORKBOOK ILLUSTRATOR	• Bonnie Shields (Tennessee Mule Artist, "A real ASS...ET")

PHOTOGRAPHERS	• Meredith Hodges (Lucky Three Ranch, Inc.) • Ann Clarke (Personal Promotion Specialist) • Jim Digby (Loveland, CO) • Pam Olsen (Pro Photo, Pocatello, Idaho)
SPECIAL THANKS	• Rick Noffsinger (Dressage and Combined Driving Trainer/Instructor) • Sue Cole (Editor of *Mules and More* magazine) • Denny Emerson (USET/USCTA Instructor/Trainer) • Paul and Betsy Hutchins (Founders of American Donkey and Mule Society) • Steve Schwartzenberger (AQHA Judge and Trainer) • Diane Hunter (ADMS Judge and Representative) • Kent Knebel (Ambulatory Equine Service) • Jerry Banks, Farrier • Larry and Fran Howe (Bitteroot Mule Co.) • Skip and Jerri Jackson and Kids (Jackson's Jackasses) • John Zwier, Jr. (Assistant to Jackson's Jackasses) • Zethyl Gates (Loveland Museum) • South Carolina Donkey and Mule Society • Smiser Freight Company (Smiser parade mules) • Cindy Powell — Mule trainer • Katie Banks, Lanny Helzer, Jack, Kristen and Jacob Skendzel, Hal Walston — parade riders/walker/driver • Rich Clarke — Debonair dude • Cammie Lundeen — Donkey owner • Doug and Lori Blake — Donkey owner • Susan Over — Mare owner • Buddy Stockwell — Donkey owner • Willis Hamm and Co. — Cowboy Metal Products • Colorado State University Veterinary Teaching Hospital, Fort Collins, CO • Dr. Jack Anderson (Chiropractor) • Kristen & Jake Skendzel, Katlin and Jamie Nicastle, and Jaren Harris (kids) • Kristen Skendzel ("Lil' ass" demo rider) • Jim Schleiger (Contributing videographer) • Jack, Renée, Dana, J.J., and Andy Anderson • Larimer County Mule Show, Loveland, CO • Loveland Museum, Loveland, CO • Abbe Ranch Horse Trials and Clinics, Larkspur, CO • Bishop Mule Days, Bishop, CA • Tricia Jones (Contributing photographer) • Pam Olsen (Contributing photographer) • Lucky Three Ranch Mules

SPECIAL APPRECIATION

My heart-felt gratitude to the following for being open-minded enough to include my mules and me in their clinics and seminars, and for helping us to achieve our dreams:

- Lindy Weatherford
- Dolly Hannon
- Rick Noffsinger
- Jack Pattison
- Major Anders Lindgren
- Jim Graham
- Denny Emerson
- Bruce Davidson
- Karen Bjorn
- Susan McLean
- Bob Loomis
- Steve Schwartzenberger
- Al Dunning
- Monte Foreman
- Sally Swift

A very special thanks to:
- My Dad, Charles M. Schulz, for buying me my first good set of harness for my team plus giving me a lifetime of support!
- My mother, Joyce Doty, for helping me get started with mules at the Windy Valley Mule Ranch in Healdsburg, CA.
- JoAnne Lang, CMT, of Loveland, CO, for all her efforts in keeping the Lucky Three longears happy and healthy!
- Richard Shrake for his inspiration and encouragement!

Special Thanks to those whose creativity and dedication have made this video training series a reality!!
- Maury Willman
- Ann Clarke
- Blake Miller
- Robbie Aukerman
- Michelle McIntosh
- Tony Servin
- Scott Collins

Getting Started

Welcome to what we hope will be a wonderful experience in mule or donkey training. You are about to learn a logical approach to working with longears.

VIEWING THE TAPES

If you purchase the videotapes in the series, ***Training Mules and Donkeys: A Logical Approach to Longears***, take the time to view each tape before you begin your training sessions. This will help you make sense of the entire process and logical order of the lessons. You will see the "big picture" and become more comfortable with terminology and techniques before you use them. **If you jump ahead or skip some of the pointers, you may find your training less effective**.

All of the information from each of the videotapes (along with additional information in many cases) is included in this book, as well as in the individual workbooks accompanying each videotape. This allows you to watch the videotapes without taking any notes. Be sure to refer to the list of equipment needed for each lesson, which can be found at the beginning of each major section (Parts 8-10) of this book.

Part 8 of this book corresponds to Videotape #8, Part 9 corresponds to Videotape #9, and Part 10 of this book corresponds to Videotape #10. (Videotapes #1 through #7 are summarized in the spiral bound book, *Training Without Resistance: From Foal to Advanced Levels.*)

WHERE TO TRAIN

The training process will be faster and easier if you train your animal in a comfortable and safe environment. Throughout the videotapes, it is recommended that you use a roundpen, arena, or obstacle course. We realize that not everyone has access to those facilities, but we suggest you work in a safe and practical environment that fits your particular situation. We will also make suggestions about how to modify training areas when appropriate.

FIELD CARDS

Each video in the videotape series comes complete with a set of field cards. These cards have been specifically designed to correspond with each volume and chapter, and contain the information that we feel is important to have handy when you are working with your mule. You can't take your VCR out in the field, but these cards are a great way to keep the information in the videotapes at your fingertips.

TIPS AND SECRETS

- Mules need patience, kindness, and understanding from their trainers. If you begin working with your mule while he is young, you are more likely to succeed with his training.
- Never get in a hurry.
- When you own a mule, think of it as a partnership, with your mule as a voting partner.

- Develop confidence and trust with your mule by being organized, consistent, and fair in your approach.
- Keep your voice unintimidating.
- Become familiar with the face tie restraint; it is a good, humane aid for difficult mules. Do not use it on horses!
- Be generous with your rewards.
- In each training session, review everything previously learned before moving on to anything new.
- Don't expect perfection every time; keep your expectations reasonable and realistic for your mule's level of training.
- Be sure your mule is quiet and comfortable with what he has learned before moving on to anything new.
- Don't drill your mule. If he isn't "getting the picture," go on to something else and come back to it in the next lesson. Short, frequent lessons are better than long drills.
- Driving a horse or mule is very different from riding. The details are more important, and it's much more difficult to learn the basics.
- Driving can be very dangerous, no matter how experienced you are.
- The grain reward is a supplement to the daily allotment of feed; do not overfeed your animal.
- Practice handling reins to teach your hands to be light and coordinated.
- Keep your cues as subtle as possible to encourage "lightness" of response.
- Never try to do an exercise any faster than you can execute it accurately.
- Anytime your mule gets strong or disobedient, stop and back him.

Special Offer

Thank you to all who have shown such great enthusiasm for the videotape series and book! In appreciation, if you purchase at least seven videotapes, your next tape is $20.00 off.

Website

And, hey, the mules are surfin' the Internet! Check the home page for the Lucky Three Ranch:

www.LuckyThreeRanch.com

E-mail questions to Meredith at:

lucky3@willman.com

TABLE OF CONTENTS

Note: This workbook begins with Part 8 which corresponds to Videotape #8. Parts 1 through 7 are covered in a separate workbook, *Training Without Resistance: From Foal to Advanced Levels* and in Videotapes #1 to #7 of the videotape series, ***Training Mules and Donkeys: A Logical Approach to Longears***.

PART 8

MANAGEMENT, FITTING, AND GROOMING

Volume 1: Management

Volume 2: Preparing for the Show

EQUIPMENT NEEDED

Proper equipment is crucial to success in training your mule or donkey. For Part 8 and Videotape #8, you will need the following equipment:

1. Halter with lead shank
2. Lunge whip
3. 16' twisted rope for scotch hobbling
4. Shelter (loafing shed, barn, stable)
5. Trough, water bucket, automatic waterers
6. Muck bucket, manure pick, shovel, broom
7. Grooming tools (rubber curry comb, dandy brush, body brush, hoof pick, mane and tail comb, sweat scraper, grooming cloth)
8. Oster™ A-5 clippers, size 10 blades, large animal clippers, and scissors
9. Shampoo and conditioner
10. Baby oil
11. Vacuum cleaner with hose
12. Braiding materials (small rubber bands, mane comb, scissors, hair spray, braid puller, yarn, separator, seam ripper)
13. Black or clear hoof dressing
14. Show halters for English or Western
15. Dressage or driving whip
16. Showmanship attire, both English and Western
17. Riding gloves and boots

First Aid and Vet Kit

1. Sturdy box to hold your materials
2. Stethoscope
3. Large roll of cotton
4. Duct tape
5. Gauze pads and gauze wrap
6. Vet wrap
7. Disposable gloves
8. Metal twitch
9. Furacin™ Dressing
10. Phenylbutazone (tablets or paste)
11. Banamine™
12. Sterile syringe (large and small)
13. Various sized needles
14. Betadine™
15. Saline solution
16. Equine thermometer
17. Clippers with surgical blade
18. DMSO (Dimethylsulfoxide)
19. Tri-Tec 14 fly repellent
20. Kopertox™
21. Neosporin™ ointment
22. Panalog ointment

PART 8

MANAGEMENT, FITTING, AND GROOMING

INTRODUCTION TO MULES AND DONKEYS

Whether you want a backyard pet for your children to grow up with, a reliable pack animal to help you enjoy the high country, or something flashy for the show ring or dressage arena, you want an animal that will perform in a safe, obedient manner. The videotapes in this series, created by renowned mule expert, Meredith Hodges, are designed to help you understand mules and donkeys, and learn how to handle and train them correctly. The result will be a beautiful, well-mannered, well-trained, modern mule!

ABOUT MEREDITH HODGES AND THE LUCKY THREE MULE RANCH

Since 1973, Meredith Hodges has been dedicated to the positive promotion of longears. At the Lucky Three Mule Ranch in Loveland, Colorado, she began breeding a line of mules of exceptional quality and athletic ability.

In 1984, *Lucky Three Sundowner* became the World Champion Reining Mule at Bishop Mule Days in California. In 1986, Meredith successfully introduced mules to the world of dressage and show jumping.

Meredith is a respected authority as a riding and training instructor, breeder, and promoter of mules and donkeys. She has performed in numerous reining, dressage, and jumping exhibitions and demonstrations at major horse and longears shows since 1984.

Meredith wasn't always obsessed with longears. Starting out as a horse nut back in 1973, Meredith was recruited by her mother, Joyce Doty, to help on her sprawling 1000-acre Windy Valley Ranch in Healdsburg, California. She was assistant trainer for sixty broodmares, seven jacks, six jennets, and she trained an average of twenty-five mules per year. After about three months, she became infected with a "terminal case of mule fever"—an affliction from which Meredith proudly says most people never recover.

Since 1980, Meredith has owned and operated her own breeding and training farm for top-quality donkeys and mules, producing numerous World Champions. Besides competing in champion mule events, Meredith rode *Lucky Three Sundowner* at 3rd Level Dressage in two world championships; she rode *Mae Bea C.T.* to a second and later a first place at the Abbe Ranch Horse Trials.

In addition, *Lucky Three Ciji* was named Champion by the International Sidesaddle Organization, she was the national and international Reserve Champion Mule, and the World Champion Sidesaddle Mule at Bishop Mule Days in 1992.

Meredith's donkey jack, *Little Jack Horner*, jumped over 3'6" feet in exhibition at Bishop Mule Days to become the only formal jumping donkey in the world.

Meredith took three mules, including the dressage mule, *Sundowner*, to the Tournament of Roses Parade in Pasadena, California. At the opening night ceremonies for the Colorado Classic Horse Show in Denver, Meredith and her daughter Dena, gave exhibitions in pas de deux jumping and bridleless jumping. Meredith rode *Mae Bea C.T.* sidesaddle in the 1993 Inaugural Parade in Washington, D.C.

Since 1980, Meredith has been an animal inspector, representative, and judge for the American Donkey and Mule Society (a national organization). She has written Mule Crossing since 1983, a column appearing in over twenty equine publications internationally.

Her beautiful hardbound book, *Training Mules and Donkeys: A Logical Approach to Longears*, was published in January, 1993. She followed the book with a series of ten professionally-produced videotapes from 1997 to 2000. Meredith is frequently invited to share her expertise at conferences, workshops, seminars, and shows.

She has lectured at the Michigan Horse Expo in Lansing, Michigan—her seminar was the most well attended at the Expo. She has judged numerous shows including those in Haines, Oregon; Dallas/Fort Worth, Texas; Odessa, Texas; and at the North Carolina State Fair.

Many articles have been written about the Lucky Three Ranch including:

- October 6, 1986: "Mules Do More Than Pack," *Fence Post*, Bellvue, CO.
- March 1987: "Mules Make The Grade," *Equus*, Gaithersburg, MD.
- March 20, 1989: "Jumping Longears," *Fence Post*, Bellvue, CO.
- May 1990: "Sport Mules," *Horseplay*, Gaithersburg, MD.
- September 1991: "Leaving The Plows In The Fields," *Reporter-Herald*, Loveland, CO.
- September 1992: "We've Come A Long Way," *Bit and Bridle*, Bellvue, NE.
- May 1993: "Longears In High Society," *Sports Illustrated*, New York, NY.
- March 1996: "Mule InterView Points," *Western Mule*, Lebanon, MO.
- May 1996: Centerfold photograph in *Stable Kids*, Grand Island, NE.

WHAT MEREDITH SAYS ABOUT MULES

According to Meredith, "Mules are wonderful animals—strong, intelligent, affectionate, and with a great sense of humor. And what incredible athletes! But training a mule or donkey is different from training a horse. When people say 'stubborn as a mule,' they're making a mistake! In order for training to be successful, you need to fully understand the horse-half of the mule and the donkey-half as well."

What Makes a Mule Different from a Horse?

Let's clarify what a mule is first. A mule is the offspring of a male donkey (a jack) and a female horse (a mare).

A horse has 64 chromosomes and a donkey has 62. The mule ends up with 63 chromosomes. Mules can be either male or female, but because of the odd number of chromosomes, they can't reproduce. A male mule should still be gelded to make him a safe and sociable animal.

Other than the long ears, mules look very similar to horses, but there are other, not so obvious, differences. For example, the muscle composition of mules is different from that of horses—mules have smoother muscles. Comparing the muscling of horses and mules is like comparing the build of a football player to that of a ballerina. Both are very strong but the mule, like the ballerina, has more endurance and greater physical strength for its size.

A mule gets its athletic ability from the horse and its intelligence from the donkey. Donkeys and mules have been labeled "stubborn" for centuries, but they are really displaying an abundance of common sense and a strong desire for self-preservation that is often misinterpreted.

Mules and donkeys have a natural attraction to humans. When treated with patience, kindness, and understanding they learn to trust and obey. If they are treated with pain and abuse, they are not likely to comply with your wishes.

If only a mule could talk, most people would be very surprised at how smart they really are!

COMMONLY ASKED QUESTIONS ABOUT MULES AND DONKEYS

1. What is a mule?

    Mule refers to a cross between two species of equine: the horse or pony (*Equus caballus*) and the domestic donkey (*Equus asinus*). The mule's conformation falls somewhere between that of the donkey and that of the horse. A mule inherits the best qualities from the sire and the dam: its athletic ability comes from the horse and its strength and intelligence comes from the donkey.

    Mule is the term used for either the cross of a male donkey with a female horse or a male horse with a female donkey, although the latter is more correctly known as a hinny.

    Both mules and hinnies have one horse and one donkey parent; however, the two crosses generally differ from each other in appearance and stature and, to some extent, in temperament.

    The hinny has been used as a saddle animal from antiquity and is more difficult to produce than the mule because the typical jennet does not conceive well to the stallion. Certain breeds of mares do not conceive as well as others with the jack.

    - Jack + mare = mule.
    - Stallion + jennet = hinny.
    - Donkey + zebra = zebrass.
    - Male mule = horse mule or john mule.
    - Female mule = mare mule or molly.

2. Can a mule reproduce?
    - Hybrids are usually not fertile.
    - Although hybrids are typically sterile, there are two documented cases of fertility: Old Beck and Krause. There are no documented cases involving fertile male mules.
    - Mules are also used for equine embryo transplant.
    - Jack + mare mule = jule or donkule.
    - Stallion + mare mule = hule.

3. What is the history of mules in the United States?
    - Coronado is said to have used pack mules in his explorations in 1540, as did other explorers of the New World.
    - The father of our country, George Washington, was also the father of mule breeding in the Americas. He tried to purchase some jacks from Spain, but a law disallowed the selling of jacks because of their prized value. When the King of Spain learned that the President of the U.S. wanted to purchase Catalonian jacks (considered the finest jacks in the world), he gave Washington two jacks and two jennets. During the ocean crossing, one of the jacks died.
    - The jack that lived was named Royal Gift and became the foundation sire of the modern mule in the United States. Royal Gift arrived at Mount Vernon in 1785.
    - By the 1830s, Kentucky breeders had produced high-quality mules by crossing jacks with Thoroughbred and draft mares.
    - Missouri, Tennessee, and Kentucky have always been the primary mule-producing states.

- During the height of horse and mule production in the U.S. (in 1925), there were three classes of mules: the draft mule, the Southern mule, and the mini-mule.
- The draft mule was usually produced by crossing a mammoth jack with a Belgian or Percheron mare. These mules were usually 15 to16 hands high, weighed between 1,200 and 1,400 pounds, and were most often used in the northern states.
- The Southern or cotton mules resulted from a cross with a lighter mare. They weighed between 900 and 1,200 pounds and were used for cultivation, for packing in the mountains, and for riding.
- The mini-mule was produced by breeding to very small mares or pony mares and was often used in the mines.

4. Where did donkeys originate?
- Descended from the Nubian wild ass of North Africa.
- Related to both the zebra and the horse.
- Similar to the Somali wild ass which has leg stripes.

5. What sort of animal is the wild ass?
- Desert dwelling animal with great tolerance for heat.
- Able to turn feral and breed in wild herds in desert areas.
- Adapted to rocky areas with protective coloring for a harsher life.
- Extremely fleet of foot, but prefers to retreat among rocks to avoid chase.
- Tends to freeze when in danger rather than flee—a quality that has been mistaken for stubbornness.
- Survives on little food; able to eat coarse forage and drink water infrequently.

6. What are the physical characteristics of the wild ass?
- Typically a blue dun (ash gray) color with a dark line down the back and a dark cross over the withers.
- Occasionally have black lines on forearms and thighs.

7. What are other names for the donkey?
- Most properly known as the ass; the scientific name is *Equus asinus*.
- Ass in Spanish is asno; the translation of donkey in Spanish is burro.
- The name donkey came from England and is a contraction of the word dun (referring to color) and -ky (a diminutive).
- The name ass was brought to the U.S. by the Spaniards and is common in both North and South America.
- Jack = male donkey; jennet or jenny = female donkey.

8. What is the history of the ass?
- Used for pack caravans and for saddle from earliest history.
- Domesticated in North Africa and first used in Egypt and the Middle East. Gradually spread into Persia, through Greece, up the Balkan Peninsula, and also by sea to Sicily in southern Italy.
- Used for mule breeding after the horse was domesticated.
- Has lived in almost every country of the world.
- Population is larger in warmer countries.

- The ass has served mankind from at least as early as around 3400 B.C. It is also referred to in the Bible; in David and Solomon's time the ass was Israel's royal beast.
- Wild horses and asses once roamed together in Asia and Africa, so it is assumed that mules were produced during early times.

9. What are the physical characteristics of the ass?
   - Brays.
   - Has long ears.
   - Has a short, thin, upright mane.
   - Has hair only on the end of the tail.
   - Tends to look horselike.
   - Comes in a variety of colors, even Appaloosa.
   - Hooves are narrow and box-like, upstanding, and made for rock and mountain climbing. They are tough and elastic, non-chipping, and can grow to long lengths when an animal is on soft ground and left untrimmed. Their hooves are very different from those of horses.
   - Body is long; muscles are long and wiry.
   - Back is short and straight, lacks upstanding withers, and is excellent for packing and bearing weight.
   - Bone is dense and hard.
   - Gestation is 12 months, whereas the gestation period for a horse is 11 months.
   - Usually has a white belly, muzzle, and circles around the eyes

10. What are the mental characteristics of the ass?
    - Highly intelligent, alert, curious, and affectionate when not affected by negative conditions (such as cruel treatment, poor shelter, poor food and water, or overwork).
    - Quick to learn. A well-trained ass is calm, tolerant, loyal, affectionate, obliging, and patient.
    - Can be mistaken for stubborn when it is actually afraid or confused.
    - Has common sense and is not prone to panic or carelessness.
    - Can recognize danger.
    - According to Tom Constantino, "Jesus chose a donkey colt, unridden, uninfluenced by man, for his triumphant entry into Jerusalem on Palm Sunday. In doing so, he recognized the donkey's instinctive role of servitude to man and God. Time and time again since the beginning of recorded history, the donkey has proved its quality of character. Its noble instincts are special. It was not created to be hunted for food or sport, and it has no natural enemies. It is the duty of the world to understand the true depth of the donkey, and to care for this noble creature."

11. What are the size divisions of donkeys and mules?
    - Miniature: 36 inches or less at the withers.
    - Small Standard: 36.01 to 40 inches.
    - Standard: 40.01 to 48 inches.
    - Large Standard jennets: 48.01 to 54 inches. Large Standard jacks: 48.01 to 56 inches.
    - Mammoth jennets: 54.01 inches and over. Mammoth jacks: 56.01 inches and over.
    - Division by size rather than breed is due to unclear ancestry in the New World. Donkeys were turned loose by explorers and interbred.

12. Where are donkeys and mules registered?
- Today donkeys and mules are registered in several different registries, the largest of which is the American Donkey and Mule Society.
- Other registries include the American Mule Association, the Standard Jack and Jennet Registry (SJJR), and NASMA.

MULE CONFORMATION

The following are descriptions of the ideal conformation traits of the mule. A good knowledge of conformation is necessary for selection and proper care and use of your mule.

Head
- Prominent, pleasant features are desirable.
- Eyes should be soft, kind, and large and should reflect health and intelligence.
- Ears should have length and be nicely tapered.
- Nostrils should be relatively wide to accommodate respiration during workouts.
- Forehead should be broad, medium boned; a Roman nose is optional.
- Length of head should be proportionate to body size and slightly longer than that of a horse.
- Muzzle should be small and delicate with a shallow mouth and well-aligned teeth.

Neck and back
- Neck should have good length and sit well back on the shoulders. It should not be excessively arched or u-shaped.
- Withers should be apparent, but they will not be as prominent as those of a horse.
- Back should be medium length (often shorter than a horse) and nearly straight across the top line. It should show strength over the loins.
- Croup is rounded, tapering to the tail, which indicates staying power and strength.
- Muscling should be smooth.
- Tail should not be set either too high or too low.

Shoulder
- Long, sloping at nearly a 45-degree angle; it will be slightly steeper than that of a horse.
- Broad collar surface.

Barrel and hip
- Ribs should be well sprung, extended, not full.
- Ribs should end close to the hip bone.
- Flank and barrel should be well set down with a flat appearance, not indented.
- Hip, stifle, and gaskin should all have a smooth muscle appearance. They should not bulge.

Chest
- Chest should be deep and prominent.
- Chest should be broad and well developed.
- Chest should resemble a turkey's breast with one smooth muscle (no clear line of separation as in horses).

Legs and hooves
- Legs should be nearly straight with a broad, clean, large bone, but not meaty.
- Legs should be well braced from all quarters and inner joints; set properly underneath him.
- Knees should be broad, deep, and firmly set.
- Hocks should be broad and muscular; slight cow-hocking in mules is common.
- Forearms and stifles should be well developed with muscles tapering to knees and hocks in regular, well-defined lines; muscles should not bulge.
- Hooves should not reflect a ribbed appearance; they should be smooth and look sleek and oily.
- Hooves should not be contracted, but well sprung and supported; they are smaller than those of a horse of the same size. Frogs should be well extended and healthy.
- The old saying, "no foot, no horse" is literally true in the mule, as in any other animal used for travel.

Coat and hair
- Hair should be soft and shiny, covering a pliable skin.
- The coat should be soft to the touch; this denotes good fattening qualities.
- Colors vary, but a lighter color can be found on the muzzle, around the eyes, on the belly, and inside the tops of the legs; the mane and tail may be darker.
- Often a donkey 'cross' (dorsal and wither stripe) and sometimes zebra stripes can be found on the shoulder and legs.
- Colors include light bay, chestnut, and black, all occasionally with white socks and/or white face markings.
- Other colors may be white, roan, piebald, or skewbald, though these appear infrequently.

Voice
- The voices of mules and hinnies are different from each other and from horses and donkeys.
- Mules, because they typically are more active and outgoing, call more than hinnies.
- A mule's voice is more like that of a donkey than a horse, making a sound on both exhalation and inhalation.
- A mule's voice ranges from a 'bawl' to a squeal to a horse-like whicker.
- Hinnies seem to call when very upset, making squealing noises.

BASIC MULE CARE

- Mules are cheaper to keep than horses
- They are more durable animals and are more resistant to parasites and disease.
- They require less feed and lower protein to maintain good health.
- They are intelligent in potentially dangerous situations and will avoid harm to themselves.
- They require less hoof care than horses in many instances. Under reasonable conditions trims are sufficient. Shoes are not necessarily needed.

Shots

Shots are given based on your geographic location—consult your local veterinarian before proceeding.

- Four-way vaccine
- Rhinopneumonitis
- Potomac horse fever vaccine
- Main shots are given in spring, one time
- Booster shot in fall

Worming

Animals should be wormed every eight weeks, starting at birth. Check with your veterinarian for varied worming schedules to prevent immunity to worming.

Feet

Check with your farrier. Conditions such as activity level, terrain, and health status may dictate different trimming and shoeing needs. In general, mules should be trimmed or shod every six to eight weeks. When a foal is one to two months old, begin to consider trimming his feet as your farrier recommends.

Teeth

Check the foal's wolf teeth while he is still nursing. Wolf teeth are tiny canine teeth in the space in front of molars. If not removed, they may interfere with the bit and cause considerable pain for your animal. In addition, have your veterinarian check the teeth regularly to determine if they need to be floated.

Chapter 1   Housing Your Mule

Owning an animal is a heavy responsibility. This video is designed to give you sound information about this complex job. In general, the principles of good management are the same everywhere, and they apply whether you own one mule or a dozen.

Let's start with the basics: shelter. Your mule doesn't ask for much in the way of shelter. He needs protection from the winter winds, a bit of shade in the summer, and a dry spot out of the rain and snow. A loafing shed in a pasture can accomplish this very easily. The shed doesn't need to be fancy but should be well constructed for safety, and arranged so it can be kept clean. In Colorado, our pasture sheds face the south for warmth in winter and protection from the wind.

Keep baling wire and twine picked up, and eliminate any trash and junk from the area in which you keep your mule.

Stalls: For those mules fortunate enough to live in a barn or stable, here are some basic considerations. The size of a box stall should be 10' by 10' to 12' by 12'. If you're foaling a mare, a much larger stall is essential. The ceiling should be at least 8' high. Doors should be 4' wide. Stalls should be well lighted with lots of fresh air and ventilation.

Tie Stalls: Tie stalls should be no less than 5' wide and 12' long, including the manger.

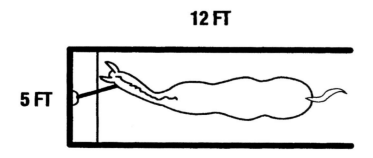

Grain Box: Construct the grain box so it can readily be cleaned, and the hay manger so chaff, dirt and debris can be easily removed. Make sure both feed and water are placed high enough to avoid contamination by manure.

Water: In the stalls and in the pens, locate the water source far enough away from the hay and grain that it will stay clean and free of debris.

Stable Floor: The stable floor should be higher than the surrounding area so it will stay dry. The surface might be anything from wooden planks to packed clay, and some people cushion the hard floors with rubber mats.

Bedding: Adding an absorbent surface material will make your mule more comfortable and will help with cleanup chores. It will also make it easier to keep your mule clean! Bedding varies according to the part of the country in which you live, but it should not be dusty, too coarse, or too easily kicked aside.

Straw or shavings generally make the best bedding. Shavings should be of pine or other woods non-toxic to equines. Pick your bedding with an eye not only to cost and absorbency, but to compost value also. After all, you've got to do something with that manure you muck out every day, so treat it as a "crop" that will eventually enrich your pasture or someone's garden.

Mucking-out tools: Speaking of mucking out, here are the tools of your trade: a muck bucket and a manure pick. You should plan to remove manure and wet bedding daily. Use a shovel and a broom for thorough cleaning.

Fencing: Regardless of where you keep your mule, you must always be alert for loose boards, nails, and anything that can cause a cut or an injury. The safest fencing is constructed of pipe or plastic-lined boards.

Wooden fencing is also safe but it won't take you long to discover that mules love to chew the wood. If you're stuck with wood, you can help preserve your fences by running a hot wire along the inside of the fence.

Wire fences, especially barb wire, cause many injuries, especially to youngsters. A smooth top wire or a board or pole fastened to the top of the fence is safer. Check fences regularly and keep them tight and in good repair.

Chapter 2   Feed and Nutrition

Feed is the most important factor influencing your mule's health. You feed for many purposes: maintenance, growth, fitting, reproduction, lactation, and work.

Hay, grain, pasture, vitamins, minerals, salt, and water must be available in the proper quantity to supply the nutrients needed by your mule. Your job is to plan a feeding program that will furnish all the required nutrients.

For now we'll talk about an average saddle mule. You'll want a good covering of flesh but not an overly fat body condition. And balance your feeding with exercise to keep the body hard and the mule's muscles in good tone.

Access to a healthy, well fertilized pasture is one of the cheapest and best ways to feed your mule. You can supplement your mule's energy requirements as needed with hay or grain. Mules do quite well on good quality grass hay, or an alfalfa-grass hay mix.

Hay should be early cut, leafy, bright green, fine-stemmed, well-cured, and free from weeds, dust, and mold. Timothy and other grass hays are preferred by most horsemen because they are easy to harvest and cure, and are easily digested. They are a bit low in protein compared to alfalfa.

Most horse pellets and hay cubes are made from alfalfa because it is high in protein and a good source of vitamins and minerals, but remember that a mule does not require as much protein as a horse.

Feed only good quality hay and grains that are free from dust and mold. If dusty hay must be fed, you should sprinkle it with water to keep the dust down. In case you haven't guessed, feeding horses and mules is both an art and a science! It is generally recommended that you feed about a pound of grass hay for each 100 pounds of body weight. When feeding alfalfa hay, cut back to about half that amount.

At the Lucky Three Ranch, our mules get about two pounds of crimped oats each day during the colder months or during training. During the warmer months or when not in training, they get only 1 pound each day. If you're used to feeding a horse, this might sound inadequate, but mules have different energy requirements than horses. A mule does just fine on less grain, and he won't do well at all on the sweet feeds that horses often eat. A mule can founder on a sweet feed because it's just too hot.

Mules and horses are more likely to suffer from lack of calcium and phosphorous than from any other mineral except salt. One of the best ways to make sure your animal is getting the vitamins and minerals he needs is to feed a good commercial supplement. Also, some people keep a free-choice mineral block handy.

Salt for a grass-eating animal is more than just a condiment—it's an essential nutrient, and it's almost always deficient in diets of mules and horses. Make sure your mule has free choice of a constant supply of iodized salt. It's amazing to note that an animal needs from one to three ounces a day, depending on the weather and work! And our mules always get an ounce of corn oil for shiny coat and digestive tract regularity.

Whatever the selection of hay and grain, remember that a mule's stomach is designed for almost constant intake of small quantities of feed, such as when he's grazing on pasture. A large quantity of feed all at once is unhealthy and unnatural. It would be ideal if you could feed your mule small quantities three times a day, at morning, noon, and night.

Plan to feed at least twice each day—once in the morning and once in the evening. Make sure you feed at the same time each day. Mules are like people—they love routine and will tell you in no uncertain terms if you're late with their supper!

Lastly, keep fresh, clean drinking water on hand at all times. Your mule will drink 10 to 12 gallons a day, and even more in hot weather or at work.

You must watch your mule to see how he holds his condition. Each animal is different—like people—and will need slight changes in feed to keep in condition. Use your eyes: look for shiny hair, bright eyes, good body flesh, a happy attitude, and healthy manure.

One of the best examples of how feeding and exercise combine can be seen in a halter class. You may not be able to do much about your mule's conformation, but you can certainly affect his muscling and conditioning. Exercise is necessary to build muscles and develop wind.

Your mule should receive some planned exercise each day. Training and exercise can be combined, but keep them in balance. Your mule should be getting 45 minutes of training several times a week, but between training sessions get him out for long, relaxed trail rides where he can walk and trot out.

Walking builds muscles; trotting builds muscles and develops wind; loping will develop wind. A good guide might be to walk for 45 minutes, trot for 10 minutes, and lope for five minutes. A mule too young for riding can be lunged for fitness and conditioning. As he becomes better conditioned, you can add cavalletti rails in the roundpen to increase the intensity of his work.

Chapter 3   Health and Routine Care

Your mule depends upon you for his safety and well-being. The best feed in the world won't keep him in good health if you neglect other important areas such as vaccinations and worming. It's up to you to create a program to prevent disease and control parasites. Here are some suggestions for a general health program.

Cleanliness is very important. Make sure feed boxes are clean and manure is removed from stalls and paddocks. Do not feed hay or grain on the floor or anywhere it may become contaminated with manure. Similarly, small, heavily used pastures tend to build up a heavy parasite load. Pastures should be rotated and harrowed as frequently as possible to break the life cycle of the parasites.

Internal parasites are the most common danger to the health and well-being of your mule, and you must be prepared to wage a constant battle to control these worms. Follow your vet's advice to set up a parasite prevention and control program through regular wormings. The drugs available today are very effective in removing parasites and breaking the cycle of reinfection. At the Lucky Three Ranch, we worm every two months.

And don't forget to watch for bots and remove them immediately.

Avoid letting your mule drink from public watering facilities. Use your own clean water buckets. Keep an eye out for anything that might injure your mule and remove or repair it.

Proper treatment of diseases and injuries depends on two very important factors: correct diagnosis and knowledge of the proper treatment. Your job is to become familiar with symptoms of diseases. In case of sickness or injury, know what to do before help can arrive. Understand what simple treatments and remedies are safe to follow. Above all, know when to call a veterinarian.

There are many resources available to help you learn how to be better prepared including books, clinics, and especially advice from an expert such as your own vet.

Assemble your own equine first aid kit and learn the proper use of each item in the kit with the help of your veterinarian. Be prepared to handle the situation before the vet arrives.

When signs of infectious disease appear, isolate affected animals promptly and call your veterinarian.

Seek your vet's recommendations for shots and immunizations, and faithfully follow an annual vaccination program. Make sure you keep good records of vaccinations and wormings, and be sure to keep track of when they're next due.

One of the best ways to monitor your mule's health is by establishing a daily grooming routine. Not only will he be rewarded with a shiny coat but you can watch for cuts and bruises and check the condition of the feet.

Basic grooming tools include a rubber currycomb to rough up the hair and bring dirt to the surface, a dandy brush to lift out the dirt, a body brush to smooth and shine, a hoof pick to clean the feet, and a mane and tail comb. A sweat scraper is handy to remove excess water after a bath or sweat after a workout, and a grooming cloth can be used to polish the coat and bring out the shine. In the spring a shedding blade is also nice, and a sponge can be used to clean muddy legs.

Begin your routine by using a hoof pick to clean the feet. Start with the near forefoot, move to the near hind, then the off fore and off hind. If your young mule is skittish, work in whatever order he is comfortable with. As he becomes accustomed to having his feet cleaned, you can do them in the proper order. Clean from heel to toe and watch for infections like thrush and rock or nail injuries. This is also a good time to check his shoes. Mules should be shod or trimmed approximately every six to eight weeks according to use.

Next, begin to groom the body, starting on the left side at the head. Hold the currycomb in one hand, keeping the other hand free to control your animal. Gently curry in small circular strokes, working your way down and back, ending with the hind leg. Next brush vigorously. After grooming the left side, move to the right side. Brush the head, and comb and brush the mane and tail. Finish with a soft body brush. Finally, use the grooming cloth to wipe around the ears, face, eyes, nose, lips, sheath, and dock of the tail.

While paying this much attention to your mule's body, you will be sure to see anything abnormal such as an abscess, a cut, mites or insects, or a sore. Early discovery and treatment keep problems small.

Besides routine grooming, your mule should be clipped as often as needed. Clip the long hairs from the head, the outsides of the ears, on the jaw, and around the fetlocks.

Chapter 4 Bathing and Vacuuming

Mules like to be clean! Bathing every so often will make your mule look and feel better. They especially like to have all that itchy sweat rinsed off after a good workout!

I don't recommend bathing too often with soap because a mule's skin is sensitive. Soap can irritate it as well as strip away the essential oils. Most of the time a good rinse will maintain a clean, healthy coat. Of course it's essential to have a spotless animal if you're off to a show or parade.

To get your mule ready for a bath, you might want to do a little "hose training." Think about it: it's not natural for water to be coming out of that snaky thing, and you'd better explain it to your mule! Introducing your mule to the hose isn't any different from introducing him to any other kind of new experience: show him what it is, take your time, and let him think about it!

You might begin by letting him take a little drink from the hose. Then start with his feet. Talk to him constantly to reassure him. As he adjusts, you can gradually wet him all over. Once he accepts the hose, you can proceed with the shampoo. I use a mild people shampoo because a lot of horse soaps are too harsh and may dull the coat.

When bathing, as with grooming, have a certain order and stick to it each time. Use a wash mitt, a rubber currycomb or a sponge, and don't forget to wash under the tail and around the sheath. Don't get water in his ears!

After a good scrub, it's rinse, rinse, rinse! Any shampoo left in his hair may irritate the skin and will certainly dull the coat. I usually finish with a good conditioner to replace some of the oil washed away.

If you're preparing for a show, you can apply a good coat dressing that will enhance your mule's shiny coat and help keep him clean. A word of warning: don't use a product like ShowSheen™ where you or the saddle will sit. ShowSheen™ is very slick. Need I say more?

Finally, make sure your mule is in a warm, protected area to dry. You can put him on a hot walker or even use a blow dryer to speed things up.

Once your mule has been bathed and is spotlessly clean, all you need to do to prepare him for your class is a quick once-over with a vacuum. Vacuum training is like anything else: take your time and make sure your mule understands that this strange, noisy monster is not going to hurt him. Soon he will learn to enjoy being groomed by the vacuum.

VOLUME 2: PREPARING FOR THE SHOW

Chapter 1   Body Clipping

Even if you don't plan to show your mule, you might consider body clipping. If you clip in mid-April or May, you will facilitate shedding, and the hair that grows in will be more manageable than the heavy winter hair.

Plus there's a bonus: a mule or donkey won't grow hair back as quickly as a horse. Just remember that clipped animals should be stabled and blanketed during cold weather. If you do blanket your mule, you must be ready to add or remove blankets and hoods as the weather changes each day.

To body clip your mule, begin with a quick bath. Your clippers will last longer if your mule is clean. When he's dry, use your rubber currycomb to bring any dirt and dead hair to the surface. Follow with a good brushing. If it's too cold for a bath, use a vacuum to get him clean.

Begin clipping the legs, because these are usually the hardest areas to do. If he's a little difficult, don't hesitate to use the restraints you learned about in Videotape #2. Use a twisted lead rope hobble to restrain the front legs, a scotch hobble for the rear legs, or a face tie for the head.

Start with Oster™ A-5 clippers on the coronet band and fetlock, working your way up each leg. For the body, use large animal clippers. Clip against the grain of the hair. Start at the rear and work your way forward, clipping first one side and then the other. Pay special attention to the flanks, the mane, and the fuzzy areas under the belly and around the forearms and buttocks.

If your mule has a nice mane, leave it and clip a bridle path. The length of the mane and the bridle path will depend on trends in the event you are participating in. For example, in English riding, manes are kept shorter to make braiding easier, but if your event is reining, keep the mane as long as possible.

If you're packing, you might want to shave the mane for the sake of simplicity. Many people roach the foretop and bridle path, then trim the rest of the mane to .5 inch. You may trim the outside edges and backs of the ears, but leave the inside hair to prevent irritation from flies and bugs.

The tail is another area where there are many variations. I recommend applying baby oil to the base each day and letting the tail hair grow. This is a good idea if you compete in open events with horses. A second method is to shave the first two inches of the tail for a clean, well-groomed look. A third variation is to "bell" the tail in three tiers. This looks best with a thick tail.

Now you're ready to trim the head. This will include trimming the bridle path, muzzle hairs, hair under the jaw, long hairs around the eyebrows, and ears.

Lastly, remove chestnuts and ergots by soaking them with baby oil for about 30 minutes and peeling them off. If the ergots don't peel off, you may cut them off with scissors.

Now you've got a mule that looks great! It will be easy to keep him looking good with a weekly trim that should include bridle path, ears, face, and coronet bands.

Treatment of the mane varies considerably, depending on the event you plan to show in. For Western pleasure, you may want to simply band the mane so it lies flat. The tiny rubber bands can be purchased in tack shops in colors to match your mule's hair. Tradition dictates the braiding of the mane for hunters and English classes for a neat, clean appearance.

A thick, heavy mane cannot be properly braided and must be thinned until all the hairs are about 4 to 6 inches long and lay flat on the neck. This is done by pulling out the long hairs from the underside of the mane with a mane comb.

This can be a big job, and it's annoying to your mule, so limit mane pulling to a few minutes a day.

Make sure the hair is the same length from poll to withers. Don't even think about cutting it with scissors—it will just end up short but way too thick to braid.

The mane should be braided on the right side of the mule's neck. Plan ahead: a mare should wear an even number of braids, a gelding an odd number. Start braiding with the first lock of hair behind the bridle path.

You can spritz a little water and hair spray to make the hair easier to handle. The quickest way to secure the braids is using tiny rubber bands. It's also very easy to do, and it's great for one-day shows or quick changes between classes.

Sewing with thread or weaving yarn looks very professional and is more permanent, but it's also more time-consuming. Once the braid is finished it should be folded once, and fastened with either bands or thread. It can also be rolled and tacked into place. How you finish your braid will depend on the time and look you want to achieve as well as what looks good on your mule!

Braiding the tail begins with a clean, well-groomed tail. Even short hair can be braided if you use a lot of hair spray to make it sticky! Moisten all the hairs along the dock with a damp sponge and bring them forward. Take a section of hair from each side of the tail, as close to the top as possible, pulling them out from as far under as you can.

On a horse you can pick up a third section from the middle of the tail but on a mule's thin tail, take the hair from the side. Cross it over one of the outer strands. Begin braiding with three strands down the center of the tail. With each twist of the braid, pick up a little more hair from either side or the middle. Continue braiding until you reach the root of the tail, then don't add any more hair but braid until you reach the end.

Fasten the end of the braid with a tiny rubber band or a piece of yarn. Now fold the braid once and pull the end up into the braided root, tying it at the base with yarn.

Chapter 3   Advanced Showmanship

In showmanship and halter classes, it goes without saying that your mule must be groomed to perfection. This means that for months prior to the show you've given your mule a good brushing or vacuuming every day.

Brushing stimulates the skin and brings out the natural oils that make the coat shine. No amount of "shine in a can" will replace the natural luster of a mule that's been brushed each day! You can apply a little baby oil before you go into the show ring, but avoid a greasy appearance.

You can band your mule's mane to make it neat for the class and apply a black dressing on the hooves. If your mule has light-colored hooves, apply a clear polish rather than black.

Your equipment and personal dress should be neat and clean and should fit well. Make sure your attire and your tack are appropriate for the class. Most halter and showmanship classes call for a Western-style halter with a lead shank.

Occasionally you might find a "suitability for dressage" halter class or English showmanship. In that case, wear English clothing and do not show with a halter with silver trim. An English halter class calls for showing in a full bridle or a plain leather halter.

Showmanship is an art that enables you to show your mule to the judge to the best advantage. Remember, the judge wants to see your mule's conformation, soundness, and way of going. You must learn to show your mule in a manner that will bring out his natural grace and beauty as he stands or moves.

When training your mule for showmanship, use a halter with a chain lead shank. Here's how to run the chain to best control your mule:

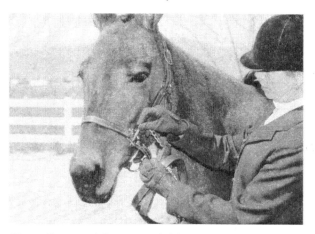
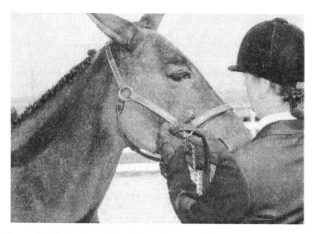

Your first goal is to teach him to walk briskly by your side, with his shoulder lined up with yours. To do this, lead from the left side with the lead shank held in your left hand about 8 to 12 inches (20 to 30 cm) from the halter. Facing forward, extend your right arm straight out in front of you and say, "walk on."

Your mule should move forward quickly and freely. Your goal is for him to move along with you, at a speed equal to yours, with his shoulder next to yours. It won't take him long to understand he is to match your pace. Practice walk, halt, walk, halt. Then add walk, trot, walk, trot. A lunge whip in your left hand can reinforce your cues to trot. Before you know it, he won't even need a lead shank—he will pace you without restraint because he understands what's expected!

Once your mule learns to walk by your side, he will need to pose for the judge. This means he should "set-up" squarely, equally balanced on all four feet. For the rest of his training and as practice for the show ring, get in the habit of holding the excess lead shank loosely in the left hand in a figure-eight coil for safety, never loose and flapping, and never wrapped around your hand.

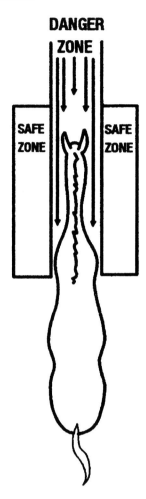

To teach your mule to set-up, walk him into position and tell him to "whoa." Make sure you stay out of the "danger zone" and pivot around to face his shoulder. Tell him to "set."

If he isn't standing squarely, show him what you want by touching his shoulder or using the lead shank to adjust his hind legs. Use small movements to avoid an overreaction. Remember that in a showmanship class you will not be allowed to touch your mule to set his legs correctly. Kicking a mule's legs into position is absolutely prohibited!

Your mule will quickly learn what "set" means. He should learn to set-up whether you are on his left or his right side. In some classes you may be asked to back your mule. You can teach him to "rein back" on command quite easily. Turn and face his chest, and pull the lead shank down and back with your right hand. If he doesn't understand, reinforce the cue by pushing intermittently on his chest with your left hand.

It won't take long for him to understand what you want him to do. When asked to back in a class, always remember to turn and face his chest, staying in the safety zone.

The last trick your mule must learn is to turn on his haunches. It is proper to turn the mule away from you, to the right, causing him to pivot in a collected, safe manner.

Hold the right arm straight, grip the lead shank close to the halter, and begin walking to the right around the mule. This will force him to turn his head and then his body within the circle you are walking.

The easiest way to school for the pivot is to position yourself next to a fence and use it as an aid. The fence will help your mule hold his pivot foot. If he doesn't turn immediately, try this trick. Hold the lead shank in your left hand and use your right hand to tap him on the shoulder or nudge him over. When he understands what's expected, switch the lead shank back to the correct position.

Here's another trick to dress up his pivot. Hold him back slightly to force him to pivot on his hind legs. A properly made 180° turn will result in your mule standing squarely in his own tracks, facing the opposite direction. It may be necessary to make your mule take a step back halfway through the turn if he is not pivoting correctly on his hind feet. When the turn is completed, your mule is now facing the opposite way. You can use 360° turns to teach him to be even more responsive.

One of the most difficult things your mule must learn is to stand perfectly still while the judge inspects him. Only by practicing with an assistant will your mule learn to pay attention to you and ignore whatever the judge might do to inspect or distract him.

Now it's time to put everything together. There are several standard patterns used for showmanship but they all have similar elements. At a show, the pattern will usually be posted before the class, but it doesn't hurt to practice a few patterns at home. You can usually count on having a judge and a ring steward in the class. The ring steward will give you instructions, but you will show to the judge. In classes with more than one judge, one will be designated the primary judge and you must ignore the others.

Begin by entering the ring at a brisk walk and look to the ring steward for instructions on where to go. Most of the time in a halter class you will walk to the judge and then trot away, but you never know what you'll be asked to do in a showmanship class, especially at the bigger shows or county fairs. The judge may be watching how you enter the ring, so make eye contact as soon as possible.

When instructed to line up, go around the back of the line and enter from the rear in the position indicated by the ring steward. Line up evenly with the others and set-up your mule quickly. Then watch the judge. Don't crowd the other exhibitors, and give yourself plenty of room so you won't get kicked.

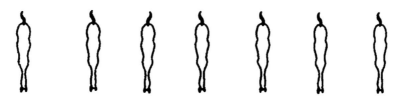

○ JUDGE

Today's halter and showmanship classes encourage the showman to stand on either side of the animal; never stand between the mule and the judge. This means you must quickly and smoothly cross in front of the "danger zone." Remember that remaining in the danger zone is a fault. If the judge is working at the front of the class, your mule should stand squarely on all four feet, with you in the safe zone on the near side, facing slightly forward. If the judge is working at the rear of the class, you may face toward the rear. To avoid blocking the judge's view, quickly move from the near to the off side of your animal.

Many breed and 4-H shows use the "quarter system" of showing so you will actually be moving from side to side in a very smooth manner while your mule stands still and the judge walks around you.

Here's a common pattern. When signaled to walk toward the judge, move out of line in a brisk, alert manner, aiming your mule, not yourself, at the judge. Halt a mule's length in front of the judge and set-up. While the judge inspects your mule, change smoothly from side to side as the judge circles.

For some breeds the judge is allowed to ruffle the mane or slip the halter back. It is then your duty to fix whatever was done, quickly and smoothly. This is when eye contact and a smile are a big part of your performance.

Upon the judge's signal to return to the line, you should execute a smart hindquarter pivot and, if directed, trot briskly through the line, executing another pivot to turn around and properly place your mule in his correct position in the line.

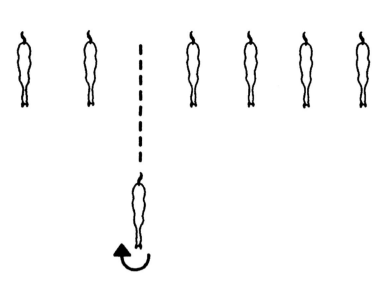

○ **JUDGE**

Another pattern might be the following. Enter and walk toward the judge. The judge will then step aside and you will trot away. Return to the line, square up, and wait for the judge to pass through the line inspecting each mule.

Still another pattern involves all competitors entering at a walk and forming a line. The judge then asks each competitor to move into a large circle, then walk and trot at his or her command. He or she will then have the exhibitors form a straight line either side-by-side or head-to-tail. Remember to leave plenty of room in your lineup for safety, and stand squarely for individual inspection.

Most showmanship or halter classes will use variations of these basic patterns. Remember that in a showmanship class, you are being judged on your ability to present your mule. In a halter class, your mule's conformation and way of going is most important. But even in a halter class, your pride and professional demeanor will help your mule stand out from the rest!

You are watched from the time you enter the ring until you leave the ring. Never assume that you are not being judged. Always keep an eye on the judge and keep your mule alert and standing squarely. Your manners and actions reflect the time and effort you have spent in preparation and training.

Never tie your mule with his show halter. Put on his everyday halter and lead rope over the show halter and then tie him.

Work calmly and quietly in the class, and keep a friendly, businesslike attitude. Even after the placings are made, the spectators are still watching you and your animal, and good sportsmanship is always appreciated.

As you can tell, there are no shortcuts to success in the show ring. Everything you do in the ring is related to everything you've done in the days and weeks and months before. The end result is the satisfaction that you've done it right and your mule is healthy and sound and has learned good ground manners. You can congratulate yourself that what you have done is admired and respected by friends and others who see you with your mule.

PART 9

Keys to Training the Donkey
INTRODUCTION AND BASIC TRAINING

Volume 1: Understanding the Donkey

**Volume 2: Measuring Your Animal
for Athletic Potential**

Volume 3: The Donkey Jack

EQUIPMENT NEEDED

Proper equipment is crucial to success in training your mule or donkey. For Part 9 and Videotape #9, you will need the following equipment:

1. **Halter with lead shank**
2. **Lunge whip**
3. **Twisted lead rope or scotch hobble**
4. **Dressage or driving whip**
5. **Riding gloves and boots**
6. **Lead shank for showmanship and for handling jacks**
7. **Splint boots**
8. **Piece of twine for measuring**
9. **Grooming kit consisting of the following:**
   - curry
   - sponge
   - mane/tail comb
   - baby oil for manes and tails
   - sweat scraper
   - dandy brush
   - finishing rag
   - hoof pick
   - body brush
   - clippers (large and small)
10. **Treat bag**

First Aid and Vet Kit

1. **Sturdy box to hold your materials**
2. **Stethoscope**
3. **Large roll of cotton**
4. **Duct tape**
5. **Gauze pads and gauze wrap**
6. **Vet wrap**
7. **Disposable gloves**
8. **Metal twitch**
9. **Furacin™ dressing**
10. **Phenylbutazone (tablets or paste)**
11. **Banamine™**
12. **Sterile syringe (large and small)**
13. **Various sized needles**
14. **Betadine™**
15. **Saline solution**
16. **Equine thermometer**
17. **Clippers with surgical blade**
18. **DMSO (Dimethylsulfoxide)**
19. **Fly repellent**
20. **Kopertox™**
21. **Neosporin™ ointment**
22. **Panalog ointment**

PART 9

Keys to Training the Donkey
INTRODUCTION AND BASIC TRAINING

VOLUME 1: UNDERSTANDING THE DONKEY

Chapter 1   Differences Between the Donkey and the Mule

You might have noticed something interesting happening in the equine world: more and more people are discovering the fun and satisfaction of owning MULES! Mules are popping up at open shows, in parades, and at driving events. They're even in the dressage arena and on the cross-country jump course!

Bishop Mule Days draws hundreds of mule fanciers each year. And more and more people are getting into the breeding of mules of all sizes, shapes, and colors! My book and video series on training mules and donkeys has sold thousands of copies all over the world. Longears are COOL!

LONGER EARS
SHORTER MANE + TAIL
NO CHESTNUTS
HOOVES SMALLER + DEEPER
BIG VOICE

M = 63   D = 62   B. Shields cei

As you know, the mule is the product of mating a horse and a donkey. And donkeys are what this section of the workbook (and Videotape #9) is all about!

Donkeys are members of the ass family, *Equus asinus*. A male donkey is called a jack. A female is called a jennet or jenny. Donkeys have 62 chromosomes, differing from horses with 64 and mules with 63 chromosomes.

Donkeys range in size from smaller than 36 inches to as large as 17 hands high. They have short hairs on the mane and tail, their hooves are small and deep, and some don't have chestnuts.

Donkeys have much larger ears than horses, and if you've ever heard a donkey bray, you know his voice is louder and more harsh than that of other equines. Donkeys are less likely to founder than other equines, and I don't know anyone who wouldn't say they were hardier and less subject to injury than horses.

Another interesting difference between horses and donkeys is the gestation period. Jennets carry their young for about 12 months and a horse's gestation period is 11 months. A horse mare carrying a mule foal by a donkey jack will also carry for 12 months.

There is a great deal of variety among donkeys just as there is among horses, and breeds are often mixed, especially in America. As a result, donkeys are most commonly designated by size rather than breeding. The smallest donkeys are called Miniatures and stand 36 inches and under. Standard donkeys range from 36.01 to 48 inches; Large Standard donkeys range from 48.01 to 56 inches; and Mammoth donkeys are taller than 56 inches.

Another huge difference between horses and donkeys can be seen in their attitudes toward training. A horse can be mastered and controlled relatively easily; a donkey must be coerced and persuaded to obey, never forced.

Donkeys and mules have been labeled "stubborn" for centuries, but it's really only an abundance of common sense and a strong desire for self-preservation.

Donkeys and mules have a natural attraction to humans and when treated with patience, kindness, and understanding, they learn to trust and obey. If they are abused, they are not likely to comply with your wishes! Although there are differences in instinct and attitude, there is very little difference in technique when training a horse, a mule, or a donkey. The keys are *patience, understanding, and a good reward system.*

Chapter 2   Imprinting for Foal and Adult

Like foals of any breed, the donkey baby needs to begin his life with imprinting. Imprinting is nothing more than getting the baby used to being around people. He's going to spend the rest of his life with human beings so he should get used to your touch, your voice, your smell, and especially your handling of him. And handling the foal the minute it's born is a wonderful way to bond with him. And it lays a foundation of trust for the training to follow!

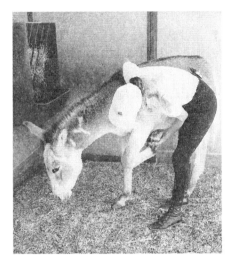

If his mother is easy to handle it will certainly help as your baby learns how to interact with humans. A calm, well-mannered mother helps produce a well-mannered foal. If your jennet is not easy to handle, then she needs training before the foal is born to assure she will be safe to be around and tractable.

When imprinting your foal, think about the kind of adult you want him to be. A donkey foal is not much different from a human baby in its emotional needs. They both need attention, love, guidance, and praise to become loving, cooperative adults. Start your relationship by creating a positive attitude. Approach your donkey with love, patience, kindness, and respect. In turn, ask him to respect you.

Like a child, a young donkey doesn't know when he's playing too rough or doing something unacceptable like nipping or kicking. You must discipline him with a firm slap, saying "No" in a firm voice. Biting warrants a slap on the side of the mouth, and kicking will get him a thump on the rump. Be consistent—those little nips might be cute right now, but without correction, they will quickly turn into an annoying, dangerous habit!

Just don't forget to reward the good behavior. By establishing a system of rewarding the good and punishing the bad, your donkey will quickly learn what is expected of him. It won't take long for him to learn to respect you, and along the way you'll notice you're creating a long-lasting bond of friendship!

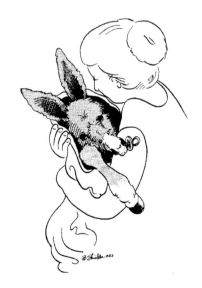

Incidentally, it doesn't matter if your donkey is a young foal or an older animal: HE NEEDS IMPRINT TRAINING!

You'll find details about how this is actually done in Videotape #1, *Foal Training*. The lessons are applicable to donkeys and mules of any age, from foal to adult. Videotape #1 also covers the technicalities of haltering, learning to be tied, leading, obstacles, and loading into a trailer. It even covers a little bit of showmanship.

As you begin your donkey's training, make sure you include an equal measure of fun. As with children, if you make learning fun, it comes more easily. Plus, you'll be cultivating your donkey's desire to please and to serve. By creating a fun, non-threatening atmosphere, you will be encouraging his enthusiasm for learning. He will want to follow you everywhere…because it's the best place to be!

One of the keys to training a donkey is this: don't be in a hurry. If you expect too much too soon, he will become overwhelmed, frustrated, and confused and he won't learn.

Compared to a horse, a donkey's response time is much slower, but his comprehension and memory retention is much greater. It might appear that your donkey is in "deep thought" for what seems to be an eternity—but he's just digesting what he's being taught. **So keep your sense of humor intact and be patient!**

Whether working with a donkey foal or an older animal, remember to take it slowly but be complete. Follow all the steps in sequence, and don't leave any step out.

Feeding time is the perfect time to scratch and pet your donkey and get him used to being handled. You can do this without a halter. Soon he will learn that he likes being with you!

After you've handled your donkey a lot then the next step, haltering your donkey, is fairly easy. Feeding time is also the perfect time to try on the halter for the first time. A safe and effective way to catch your foal is demonstrated on Videotape #1. The technique is called the "tail hold" and once you administer it, the foal will calm down very quickly. Using the tail hold you can back him into a wall so you can free your right hand and put on the halter.

Leave the halter on for a while, then take it off. NEVER LEAVE THE HALTER ON YOUR DONKEY WITHOUT SUPERVISION. A halter can be very dangerous! When your foal is used to having the halter put on and taken off, you can teach him to be tied.

This method of training outlined in Videotape #1 works well for donkey youngsters or adults. When your donkey is ready to learn about being tied, make sure you are in an enclosed arena or pen. Put on the halter and attach a thick cotton lead rope. Tie him to a stout, safe post with a safety knot. The first tie lesson should only last about 30 minutes.

Your donkey will probably figure out very quickly that he is meant to stay tied. Once he understands this lesson, you can teach him to "come" by using the methods from Videotape #1. The biggest difference between training a mule to follow and training your donkey is that the moment he follows for even just one step, feed him a reward and praise him. Stroke him on the neck, the shoulder, and the poll. Scratch his chest or rump so he knows he's doing good. Then try a few more steps.

Don't ask for any more steps each day than he is willing to give. Now, isn't this easy? You don't have to jerk and pull, you don't have to hit his rump—you just have to work with him and reward him when he does what you want!

Get in the habit of telling your donkey what you want. When you walk, say "walk." When you stop, say "whoa." Before you know it, you're ready to go exploring!

Up to this point, you've kept your donkey in a confined area such as a corral or paddock. When he leads fairly well, you can start taking walks around the farm. It's your chance to teach him to trust your judgement as you introduce him to things he might find frightening. Lead with him close to your shoulder. Step toward the obstacle as close as the lead will allow and coax him to you.

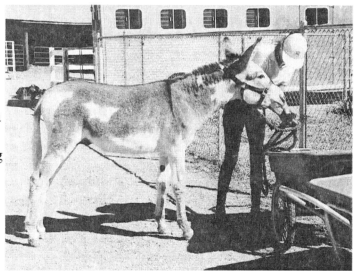

A reward might be necessary to entice him to investigate, and a reward will boost his confidence when he shows his bravery and obedience. When he's confident about investigating familiar surroundings with you, it's time to take him to the obstacle course.

Chapter 4   The Obstacle Course

An obstacle course is something you construct with safe, solid objects to teach your animals to negotiate the sorts of things they might encounter on a trail. You can start with logs spaced about a foot apart, a bridge, tires placed closely together, or any number of creative combinations. Just make sure your donkey will be safe. Let him have plenty of time to investigate each obstacle.

Encourage him to come forward, and praise him when he touches the obstacle with his nose. Teach him to trust your judgement. If he is hesitant, take a reliable "friend" along to show him that everything is all right. At first, your donkey may be reluctant to pick up his feet to go over objects. In fact, he'll probably try to go around them in any way he can! Just stand close to his head, hold him on a short lead, and ask him to "come." If he moves even just one foot over the object, stop, hold him there, and give him a reward for his effort.

Next ask for the other foot. He may just walk right over the object, and that's terrific, so reward him again. If he's still a bit reluctant, be satisfied with moving just one foot at a time. Go slow, and reward his good behavior. Be sure to use the verbal commands "come" and "whoa" in a firm manner. After all, you're establishing verbal communication that you will use for his lifetime. As you move from one obstacle to the next, approach, cue, and reward in the same way each time.

You might notice something interesting: for some reason, donkeys like to get crooked over obstacles! One way to correct this is to stand directly in front of him, grasp his halter on both sides, and control his body position as he negotiates the obstacle. This is perhaps the only time when you will violate the "safety zone" directly in front of your donkey, so be very careful and be ready to move to the side if he comes forward too quickly.

Chapter 5   Trailer Loading

The trailer is just another obstacle so you will approach it as you would any new obstacle. You can use a lunge line as a backup snub line if your donkey is a little balky, but don't get into a pulling match. The donkey will win! Just take your time and give your donkey time to think about what you are asking. If he is generously rewarded for good behavior, it shouldn't take long for him to comply. More on trailer loading can be found in my books, *Donkey Training* and *Training Mules And Donkeys: A Logical Approach To Longears*, and on Videotape #1.

Once your donkey has learned to follow you over and around obstacles, he will be ready to begin the fundamentals of showmanship.

Chapter 6   Showmanship

You can have some fun teaching your donkey to do a little showmanship. If you decide to hit a halter class at the county fair, great! But even if you never get out of your backyard, it's important that he learn how to lead properly. Plus, these lessons are the basis for more advanced training later on. Make sure he's "in showmanship training" every time you lead your donkey anywhere.

Hold the lead rope in your left hand, crossing it in front of your body. Keep your right hand free and straight out in front of you. The idea is to learn to walk and trot with slack in the lead rope and your donkey following your *shoulder*. If he gets too close, use your right hand to push him back into position. If he goes too fast, you can always use both hands to control him. Once you have begun showmanship training, ALWAYS lead him in this way. The walk from the pasture to the barn is a good place to start.

Facing forward, extend your arm forward and say, "walk on." Your donkey should move forward quickly and freely. If he doesn't, try slowing your pace to his until he comes along willingly. The goal is for him to walk along with you, at a speed equal to yours, with his shoulder next to yours. It won't take him long to understand that he is to match your pace. Once he has learned to walk with you, he must learn to stop correctly. He must stand squarely on all four feet every time he stops. By stopping "square" he is learning to hold his body in a balanced manner.

To teach him to set-up, walk your donkey into position and tell him, "whoa." Make sure you stay out of the "danger zone" as you pivot around to face his shoulder. Tell him to "set." If he isn't standing squarely, show him what you want by touching his shoulder or moving the lead shank to adjust his hind legs.

Next he must learn to trot beside you. Give the verbal command, "trot," and slowly move out at a very slow pace. I don't recommend using a lunge whip to reinforce your cue to trot. Instead, find something toward which he wants to trot. Maybe, for instance, a bucket of oats held by an assistant. You can also try enticing him with a treat in the palm of your extended right hand.

If this doesn't work, you can have your assistant follow behind with a driving whip gently reinforcing your cues as needed. As always, reward him when he responds. Above all, be patient and don't get discouraged. Remember, this is one smart fellow and he has to think this all out! If he isn't getting the idea, go back to something he already knows and does well and try again the next day. Eventually, he will get it!

I'm not going to go into a lot of detail here, because basic showmanship training is covered thoroughly in Videotape #1. Advanced showmanship training is covered in greater detail in Videotape #8, **Management, Fitting, and Grooming**. You will be taking your donkey through the same exercises outlined for a mules in those videotapes, only you must be prepared to go slower and be calmer and more supportive. Learn to reward even the slightest movement in the direction of compliance. Allow your donkey to progress at his own speed, not yours. If at any time you encounter behavior that is dangerous and unacceptable, such as kicking or striking out, by all means refer to Videotape #2, **Ground Work**. This videotape will show you how to prevent or correct nasty vices before they become a part of your donkey's behavior pattern.

The goal at this point in training is to make sure your donkey has a solid foundation in place. This means that you can put on a halter and lead and he stands quietly while you brush him and clean his feet. He follows you willingly around and over obstacles. He loads into a trailer, and he knows the basic maneuvers in showmanship. When he has mastered these small skills, he's ready for the more advanced training we will cover in Videotape #10.

VOLUME 2: MEASURING YOUR ANIMAL FOR ATHLETIC POTENTIAL

Before you invest more time and effort into training your donkey, or before you decide he will be heading to the stud barn, you should take the time to evaluate his athletic potential. The principles we'll look at now are applicable to donkeys, horses, or mules. They were developed by the famous horse trainer—and my mentor—Richard Shrake.

First, let's look at conformation. It goes without saying that he should appear well balanced and in good proportion, with flat knees and smooth joints. He should be free of unsoundness. Most breeds have published standards, or you can pick up a good 4-H manual on judging to give you an idea about what is the ideal with regard to conformation.

Next, we'll look at body measurements to gauge your donkey's athletic ability. Begin with a good length of twine or string. The first measurement is from the poll to the middle of the withers.

Then measure from the middle of the withers to the loin at the base of the rump. If these measurements are the same, you have a balanced animal. If the neck is slightly longer, he will still be athletic. But if the neck is shorter, it will be difficult for him to balance through certain movements and transitions.

Next, measure around the throatlatch. Then measure around the collar from the withers to the chest at the point of shoulder, and back to the withers. This measurement should be twice that of the throatlatch. Why? He will be better able to flex at the poll making him easier to collect and bring into the correct frame.

Now measure the top of the neck from poll to withers, and the bottom of the neck from throatlatch to chest. The top line should be 1.5 times that of the bottom to enable the animal to perform nice, soft movements. A ewe-necked animal cannot bend properly and will never be able to achieve good collection.

 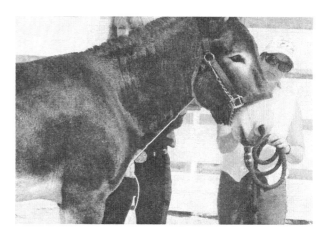

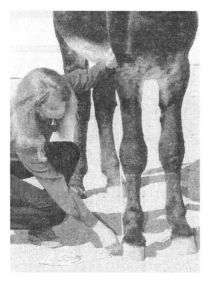 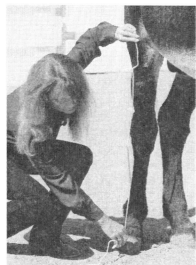 Next, measure from the elbow to the coronet band, and from the stifle to the coronet band. An evenly balanced animal will have both measurements the same. This means he will be a good pleasure prospect, with smooth movements at the walk and trot. If he's a bit longer in front, he will be a good prospect for reining, jumping, or dressage because his trot and canter will be smooth. An animal that is higher behind will find it difficult to balance and is not a good athletic prospect.

 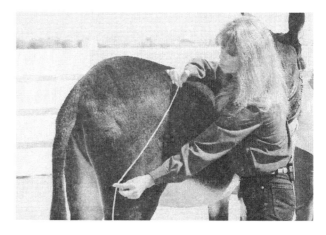

Your prospect should also be graced with 45° angles at shoulder and hip and with the same angle at his pasterns. This ideal angle will result in softer gaits and transitions. A straighter hip and shoulder will result in a rougher ride. The higher the angle, the longer the stride, and the shorter the angle, the shorter and quicker the stride.

Now let's see how your prospect moves. Stick a piece of tape at the point of his hip as a visual reference point. Have your assistant trot him on a lead as you watch. Does his hock reach underneath, and pass in front of the tape? If it does, his hindquarters will support athletic movements. His transitions will be more fluid and smooth, and his head and neck will stay level. If his hock does not reach underneath him sufficiently, he will be out of balance and must raise his head and neck through transitions.

Finally, watch him walk through smooth sand. Does his hind hoof fall into the track made by his front hoof? If he is exact, he is graced with the smooth, fluid way of going of a world-class pleasure animal. If he over-reaches the track, he has wonderful hindquarter engagement and you may have a candidate for reining or dressage. If he under-reaches the track, he is out of balance and will be raising his head through transitions and movements.

These measurements can be quite helpful in determining your animal's athletic future. They are absolutely valid—the laws of physics are at work. But as you have probably guessed, there is more to being a great athlete than just conformation. We must also look at the personality of the individual. Again, these principles apply to mules, donkeys, and horses.

First, let's look at an animal's trainability. One nice thing about owning a registered animal is that you know a lot about his gene pool. Some lines are famous for being smart, athletic, and good-natured. Some are known as being high-strung and nervous, or perhaps inappropriate for certain riders. Do your research before you look at a prospect in the catch pen.

Next are some practical tests to help you assess an animal's trainability. Have someone hold the lead rope while you pick up a handful of sand. Trickle the sand through your fingers near his head. Does he turn and look at you? If so, this is an animal who is interested in what you're doing, which means he is more trainable than one who ignores you. The animal who looks away or tries to move off is the least trainable.

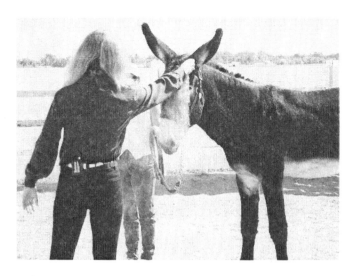

The next test is to run your finger lightly from his girth across the barrel to the flank. Do this on both sides. Does he tolerate this with little movement, or does he twitch and even flinch? This gives you an idea about how he will react to your legs when you are riding. The animal who is less touchy will be the one who learns your cues most efficiently. The one who flinches will most likely overreact.

Next stand at your donkey's shoulder and put your hand over his nose. Ask him to bend his head and neck toward you. Do this on both sides. Does he bring his nose around easily? Do you feel resistance? If he gives, he is submissive and will learn more quickly.

The final challenge is to assess your donkey's reaction under pressure. This is simple to test. Have your assistant hold the lead rope. You should make an abrupt move, like jumping and flapping your arms. What does he do? If he tries to run off, he's not the best candidate for equine sports such as driving that require a steady animal. On the other hand, if he stops to look at you and tries to figure out what you're doing, he's a great candidate for advanced training. We'll cover your donkey's training under saddle in Videotape #10.

VOLUME 3: THE DONKEY JACK

Chapter 1   Socialization

Your donkey jack is naturally warm, affectionate, and friendly as a foal. But as he reaches maturity, his hormones begin to kick in, and his natural instincts can become dangerous. It's up to you to "socialize" him and make sure he is safe and obedient with people.

It goes without saying that your donkey jack needs to lead a well-balanced life. Work, play, and social interaction help keep him calm, affectionate, and tractable.

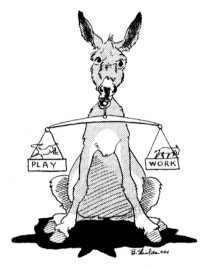

It also goes without saying that he needs a clean and comfortable place to call home. Give him plenty of space for exercise, good pasture, and adequate shelter from the elements. Fencing should be sturdy and high enough to discourage escape. A hot wire along the top rail of the fence will work well and will keep him from chewing the wooden rail.

Jacks are often used only for breeding and may spend a lot of time isolated from other animals. This might be safe, but it's not particularly good for the mental health of your jack! He needs to socialize, and he needs to work. As with any child, it's up to you to teach him proper behavior and limitations.

Feeding time is a great time to talk to your jack and handle him. Grooming is another step in his socialization.

I also recommend that you train your jack to drive or ride. At the very least, he must learn good ground manners and the basics of showmanship. It doesn't take much—just 15 minutes several days a week—and your veterinarian and farrier will thank you for your efforts!

Basic training should include haltering, leading, and learning to stand while tied. With that accomplished, you can lead him to a workstation for grooming and cleaning his feet. Walk and trot him back to his pen using the showmanship methods outlined earlier. Teach him to negotiate obstacles and move away from pressure. If you choose to give your jack more training, he will only get better!

Chapter 2　The Young Jack

If you expect to breed your jack, he should be separated from other donkeys when he is about two years old. At the Lucky Three Ranch, we separate the two-year-old jack and pasture him with a specially selected mare for an entire year. The mare should be calm, non-aggressive, and cycling regularly.

If you want a mule foal on the ground next spring, choose a younger mare. If you want your jack to simply learn to pasture breed, choose an older mare who cycles but does not conceive. The idea here is to let your jack learn to breed without the need to fight for position in a herd. This way he is less likely to become aggressive as an adult and he will be more manageable.

Some mare owners are apprehensive about pasture breeding, so it's important that your jack learn to breed in hand. You can begin this training at three years of age.

Your breeding area should be separated from other areas and equipped with either a breeding chute or a breeding pit. If the mare is taller than the jack, he may need to stand on a platform behind the chute. The mare can also be confined in a breeding pit to make her more accessible.

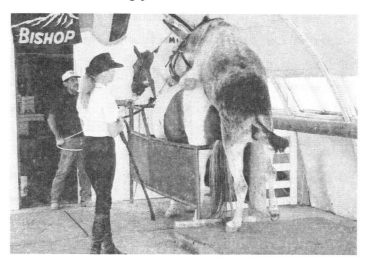

Teasing is an essential part of the breeding process, and at the Lucky Three Ranch we have a teasing stallion to do this important work. Teasing tells us where the mare is in her cycle and ensures that she is in true heat and ready to be bred. Teasing also makes her as receptive as possible to the jack.

Breeding should be a calm and deliberate experience for both the jack and the mare. The stud manager has several decisions to make, all dependent on the personality of the mare. If she is calm, she might be fine in the breeding chute and she and the jack can breed safely.

If she is nervous, the stud manager may use a twitch or hobbles during breeding. In any event, the breeding process must be safe for both mare and jack, and for the handlers as well.

After the mare has been teased, bring her to the breeding chute and settle her in. Wrap her tail. Take a clean wet cloth and cleanse her vulva. Then take the cloth and drape it on a hitch rail a few feet away from the breeding station where the jack will soon be tied. The cloth will be used to arouse the jack.

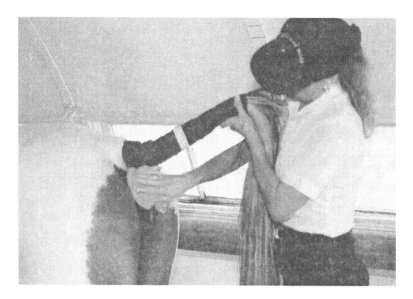

When the mare is ready, bring the jack to the breeding area and tie him to the hitch rail near the cloth. As he sniffs the cloth, his instincts will take over and it won't be long before he drops.

When he drops, wash him with plain warm water. He should be clean to begin with, but the washing is an important step before breeding can commence.

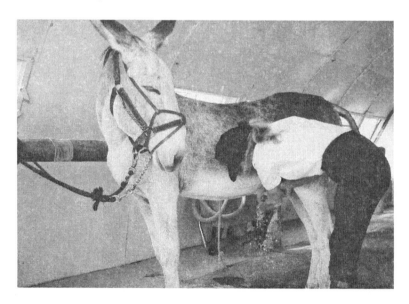

I always put a drop noseband on my jacks so they cannot bite the mare during breeding. Now you can lead the jack slowly to the mare. Allow him to sniff and nudge her, but don't allow him to be overly aggressive. If he is aggressive, don't get abusive with him, just take him back to the hitch rail and begin again.

After he has covered the mare, wash him again, reward him, and return him to his pasture or pen.

Chapter 4   Special Problems

A jack who has not been properly trained may present special behavior problems. This is often a jack over four years of age who shows aggressive behavior while you are handling or leading him, especially when he sees a mare or another jack. This behavior is dangerous and unacceptable. Sometimes a jack will not respond to corrective training and the use of stronger aids. In this case, it's time to consult a professional trainer to bring the donkey back under control.

Once your jack has learned that humans are in charge, he will learn that his hormones and instincts must be under control! Teaching him respect and obedience will only enhance his breeding and training experiences.

Throughout this workbook and the accompanying videotapes, we've talked about how training a donkey is similar to rearing a child. They both need our help to grow into reliable adults, with an investment of time and careful training. They need to learn certain rules and behavior for things to go well. You, in turn, teach them with love, patience, understanding, and just the right amount of discipline. Your donkey will bond with you during this process, and in the end, you couldn't ask for a better friend and companion!

PART 10

Keys to Training the Donkey
SADDLE TRAINING AND JUMPING

Volume 1: The Saddle Donkey

Volume 2: Advanced Training

EQUIPMENT NEEDED

Proper equipment is crucial to success in training your mule or donkey. For Part 10 and Videotape #10, you will need the following equipment:

1. **Halter with lead shank**
2. **Lunge whip**, lunge line
3. **Twisted lead rope or scotch hobble**
4. **Dressage or driving whip**
5. **Riding gloves and boots**
6. **Lead shank for showmanship and for handling jacks**
7. **Splint boots**
8. **Piece of twine for measuring**
9. **Grooming kit consisting of the following:**
   - **curry**
   - **sweat scraper**
   - **hoof pick**
   - **sponge**
   - **dandy brush**
   - **body brush**
   - **mane/tail comb**
   - **finishing rag**
   - **baby oil for manes and tails**
   - **clippers (large and small)**
10. **Treat bag**
11. **Properly fitting saddle and pad**
12. **Bridle with properly fitted bit**
13. **Crupper**
14. **Riding crop**
15. **Elbow pull made of 12-foot (4-meter) lightweight soft cotton or nylon rope with snaps on both ends**
16. **Ground driving lines or two 16-foot (5-meter) lunge lines of different colors**
17. **Materials for obstacle course and jump course**
    (See Videotapes #2 and #7 for detailed information)

First Aid and Vet Kit

1. **Sturdy box to hold your materials**
2. **Stethoscope**
3. **Large roll of cotton**
4. **Duct tape**
5. **Gauze pads and gauze wrap**
6. **Vet wrap**
7. **Disposable gloves**
8. **Metal twitch**
9. **Furacin™ dressing**
10. **Phenylbutazone (tablets or paste)**
11. **Banamine™**
12. **Sterile syringe (large and small)**
13. **Various sized needles**
14. **Betadine™**
15. **Saline solution**
16. **Equine thermometer**
17. **Clippers with surgical blade**
18. **DMSO (Dimethylsulfoxide)**
19. **Fly repellent**
20. **Kopertox™**
21. **Neosporin™ ointment**
22. **Panalog ointment**

PART 10

Keys to Training the Donkey
SADDLE TRAINING AND JUMPING

VOLUME 1: THE SADDLE DONKEY

Chapter 1   Basics in the Roundpen

The donkey is an animal born for no other purpose but to serve. If he understands what you want, he has an innate desire to please. With this in mind, be patient and know that he will learn at his own pace, but he will not forget what he has learned.

By now, you've probably noticed that your donkey is pretty darn smart! He does not forget what you teach him, no matter how many days pass between lessons. You've also noticed that as you teach him, you also learn from him. You learn to appreciate his courage and his honesty, and you learn that patience is one of your greatest assets, with a good sense of humor not far behind. Just remember that even the most well trained donkey will have his bad days or moments, but that doesn't make him a *bad donkey*.

You might be surprised to hear that your donkey will learn by just *watching* other equines being worked! It's as if he were jealous of the time spent with an animal other than himself. You can almost hear him saying, "When is it going to be my turn?" So by all means, let your donkey watch as you ride another animal! He'll be ready when it is his turn!

As you prepare for this next phase of training, be ready to spend many hours working on basic moves. Don't be disheartened if progress seems slow. Believe me, it's worth the effort!

Remember that a donkey must see a purpose for learning. You must persuade your donkey to do what you want—you cannot force him. Talk to him a lot, give him plenty of reward for his good behavior, and discipline him gently for bad behavior. Your goal is RESISTANCE-FREE TRAINING!

It is a good idea to get into the habit of using splint boots or leg wraps to protect your donkey's legs during training. A painful clip doesn't convey the right message about training, and safety is always our number one consideration.

Another good idea is to lead your donkey around the area you're going to be working in. Let him "inspect" everything and satisfy himself that there are no threats or dangers. And don't assume that because he was in the arena on Tuesday, he won't need to "inspect" it again on Wednesday. His evolutionary success was built on attention to detail, so work with him, not against him!

All of these next lessons will take place in a roundpen. Mine is 45 feet (14 meters) in diameter. It should be large enough so that your donkey can canter, but small enough that you can stand in the center and reach him with your lunge whip. If you don't have a roundpen, you can use a small square pen with four stout poles laid across the corners to make it round.

Take your donkey into the roundpen with only his halter and lead. Your first lesson will be to teach him to move away from pressure. You may have noticed that donkeys are terrific "crowders." They want to be as close to you as possible, and often this is not safe! You want to teach your donkey that he must not move into you. Sometimes it's actually helpful to put yourself between the donkey and the fence and push him toward the center.

Lead your donkey to the middle of the roundpen and ask him to "whoa." Reward him for stopping, and then step toward his shoulder, pulling his head toward you. Tap him on the flank and stifle, and ask him to "move over." You may have to use your whole body to shove him over. Keep his front end bent toward you as he steps around you in a turn on the forehand. This means his front legs remain still while his hind legs pivot around them—and you. Don't get too carried away—you only want him to take one step at each cue, so don't tap too hard. Ideally he should be crossing his near hind in front of the far hind with each step. Take it slow and reward him for each step.

When he gets the hang of it going one direction, try it on the other side. Then quit. You'll have plenty of time at the next lesson to ask for a few more steps.

When he's doing the turn on the forehand fairly easily, you can begin to teach him to move his shoulders away from you with a turn on the haunches. This is actually difficult to accomplish, because donkeys love to "glue" their front feet to the ground.

This approach is a little different from the one you would use for training a horse. Take the side of the halter in your left hand and ask for one step forward. As your donkey begins to move, push his face away from you as far as your arm will reach. With your right hand on the lead rope, gently tap him on the shoulder and give the verbal command, "over."

Remember, you want him to turn on his haunches. If his hindquarters come over, keep your left hand on the halter and put your right hand on his shoulder. Use your body weight to shove his front end over just a step. Then stop, praise, and reward him for moving his shoulders—even if you had to do all the work!

After a moment's relaxation, ask him again to move his shoulders away from you, tapping him with the end of the lead. If he turns properly, even just one step, great! Reward and praise him. If he does not respond correctly, use your body weight again to reinforce your cue. After about three tries, if he is not responding correctly, you can be pretty sure he understands what he is supposed to do—after all, you've been showing him what you want.

This is a good time to introduce him to the riding crop. The crop is an aid used when needed to reinforce a cue, and we'll be using it in all training under saddle. In this instance, use the riding crop to sharply tap your donkey's shoulder when asking for the turn. He will probably be so surprised that he'll step over very quickly. Be ready to reward him when he does and end the lesson there. At each session, ask for only as many steps as he will do easily, and quit. Your goal is to reward him for doing this simple movement correctly. Don't overdo it—the last thing you want is to encounter resistance.

Now let's teach your donkey to back. Hold the lead rope in your left hand and briefly pull down, back, and release as you give the verbal command, "back." Down, back, release, down, back, and release. If he doesn't take a step backwards, use your right hand to push and release on the middle of his chest. Use your thumb, pushing until you get a response, then instantly stop pushing. One step equals a reward, no matter how tiny the step. Ask him to back two or three more times—no more— then quit.

By now you've noticed that your donkey has his own style of learning, and his own pace. Take your time and make sure these training sessions are pleasurable for you both. You're perfecting your own style of training, and establishing a good rapport with your donkey—a rapport that will last a lifetime.

You might also notice that the one word I use over and over again is "patience." Don't expect perfection from your donkey in the very beginning. You can ask for a better response each time you work with him. It may take three or four sessions before he begins to move away from you as you want. As I mentioned before, training a donkey is a longer process than training a horse or a mule, but the end result is worth the effort!

Once your donkey has learned to move away when you ask, you can teach him to lunge. While lunging he'll learn more voice commands that will be the foundation for all his future training. But be advised that your donkey may not lunge well in a roundpen (and not at all on a lunge line) until after he is broke to saddle for all three gaits. Nonetheless, lunging helps your donkey stay fit. Lunging develops muscles, balance, and rhythm. It's also good exercise and a great way to help him stay in condition on days when you do not ride.

Go to the familiar roundpen with halter and lead rope. Make sure you protect your donkey's legs with splint boots, and have a lunge whip nearby. Begin by reviewing what he's learned so far. Then, release the lead rope from the halter. Pick up the lunge whip and hold it in your right hand. Use your left hand to point in the direction you want your donkey to travel—to the left. Raise both arms and ask him to "walk on." Make your movement big. If he doesn't move out, lower both arms and repeat the gesture and verbal command. If he still does not move out at your
command, give him a firm tap on the gaskin, just below the tail and above the hock. Now you should take a step back and let him think about what you've asked him to do.

Ideally, he will walk on with no need for another cue. If he does, praise him extravagantly so he knows he is doing what you want. If he does not walk on, repeat the process but hit the wall behind him to encourage him to move forward. Do not hit him unless he absolutely refuses to go forward. Then repeat the tap on the leg just above the hock, but only once. Then hit the wall behind him again. If he drifts toward the center, just move into him, pointing to the wall and encouraging him with the whip.

You must be careful to use the whip as a cue, not punishment. If he feels he is being punished, he will only tense up and stop. Remember that donkeys freeze when they are confused or frightened, and you will get nowhere with him at that point.

Make sure you ask your donkey to go farther each time you work with him. He's so smart, he might think you only want him to walk a few steps, then quit. In the beginning, ask him to go in one direction, and change directions with each new session. You'll teach him to reverse a little later, once he has learned what you expect.

When training your donkey, make sure you have plenty of time. You never want to be in a hurry. You want your time together to be a fun and enjoyable experience, with each of you learning about the other. Most of us today are on fast-forward. Remember that your donkey is on slo-mo!

For each training session with your donkey, review all he has previously learned. Always lead him to and from the workstation in a showmanship manner, holding the lead rope in your left hand with your right arm extended forward. Groom him and clean his feet.

Review the turn on forehand and the turn on the hindquarters in the roundpen. Send him forward to the rail in the roundpen at a walk. You may have discovered that you need to follow him more closely than you would a horse or a mule. Standing in the middle of the roundpen while you lunge may not be practical to keep him moving. Stay just behind him and to the side while driving him forward with the lunge whip, touching him with it only when absolutely necessary. Match your steps with his. Walk only as fast as he chooses. If you try to hurry, he will stop. Be sure to give the command "whoa" every time you want him to stop, and then reward him.

Now that he is moving out well at the walk, you can teach your donkey to reverse. As he walks forward in the roundpen, turn away from him, circling completely around until you are in front of him. Step toward him, lay the whip ahead of him, and give the command "reverse." Be aware of his space. Do not rush at him or he may turn improperly. You want him to turn into the rail and resume walking in the opposite direction.

Give him plenty of time to make the turn and ask him to "walk on." If he has difficulty, take a few steps forward and with the whip, tap him gently on the shoulder to encourage him to turn. There is a purpose to turning away from him rather than just running ahead of him to turn him. By turning back the opposite way from his direction of travel, you are establishing a new direction of travel, as well as giving him time to see that there will be a change in movement. Most donkeys learn this very quickly.

At this point there is often a difference between mules and donkeys. Your donkey has learned the walk and the reverse in the roundpen. Now he must learn the command to trot. Some donkeys will take exception to this command if they do not see a purpose in it.

It is time to introduce your donkey to the saddle, or the driving harness if he is too small to ride. Let your donkey see the harness or saddle and slowly put it on. Most donkeys will let you do this quite easily, without "sacking out." Just be careful when you tighten the cinch; don't make it too tight all at once.

I also introduce him to the bridle now. Press on the bars of his mouth to insert the bit and fold his ears through the headstall. Use a drop noseband to keep his mouth closed. And don't forget the splint boots.

Once your donkey is tacked up, send him to the rail of the roundpen at a walk. Then give the command to "trot" and move toward his hindquarters with the whip, shuffling your feet in the dirt to make some noise. If he trots at this point, great! Don't hit him with the whip. If he isn't trotting, use the whip once at the gaskin.

Use big motions with your arms to encourage him forward, or strike the fence behind him. Once he trots a few steps, tell him "whoa" and reward him. Ask him to trot just one more time during this session, then call it a day. Ask him to go a little farther in each training session, but ask him to trot only twice.

Once he's learned to trot, you can begin teaching rein cues. Tie the stirrups together and run the drivelines through them. Keep things simple by using a line of one color for the right rein and another color for the left. Stay consistent from lesson to lesson.

Ground drive him at a walk and do a reverse. Use the whip at the shoulder and gaskin. Remember, just a touch! Give rein cues with a gentle give-and-take, not a direct hard pull. Use the verbal cue "gee" when you want him to turn right and "haw" when you want him to turn left. Once he's letting you drive him, take off the lunge lines and send him back to the rail for trotting work.

Here's where donkey training will differ from training a horse or a mule. When your donkey is doing well at the walk with "walk-on," "whoa," "gee," and "haw," you can get ready to mount him if he is large enough to ride.

Don't forget that previous videotapes covered ground work and basic foundation for saddle, so if you need details, see Videotapes #2 and #4.

Chapter 3   Mounting

As with everything else, take this next step slowly. Check your girth one last time. Test your weight in the stirrups on both sides. If he's calm, bring your leg over his back and settle slowly into the saddle. Mount and dismount several times, and do it on both sides. If he's calm, you can stay mounted. Encourage him to bend his head and neck around to each side with light rein contact and a treat. When you're ready to move out, ask an assistant to help.

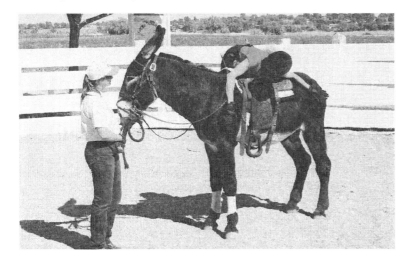

Your assistant will lead the donkey forward a few steps with you on board. Both of you should use the command to "walk-on" while you squeeze with your legs. You may use a riding crop to reinforce the cue if necessary. All you want right now is two steps! Then give him lots of praise so he knows he's doing the right thing.

Repeat this lesson each day, adding more steps, until you've gone around once in each direction. Then add "whoa" and ask for a back. To turn give light pulls on the reins—squeeze and release—with your assistant helping as needed with a hand to the donkey's chest. Then hop off and end the lesson with a brief lunge at the trot.

Donkeys learn differently from horses and mules. In the beginning, their responses are slower, but they learn completely. Once he has mastered verbal commands, rein and leg cues can be small, and the crop need be used only to reinforce a cue. How nice to discover that he responds to your verbal cues and needs minimal use of the others!

Once your donkey is at ease with you on his back, try these two exercises. Walk, halt, and back. Then walk, halt, and turn. Now your assistant can step aside and you can try the trot. Your assistant can stay in the pen to reinforce the cue, but if your donkey understands the verbal command "trot" he should quickly adapt to trotting with you on his back. Teach him to reverse. Then do figure-eights through the center.

By now, you've probably realized just how smart your donkey is! And maybe you've also noticed that he gets bored pretty quickly too. If your donkey is bored in the roundpen, perhaps it's time to take him to a more open arena and try a few patterns.

Chapter 4   Patterns and Obstacles at the Walk and Trot

Begin by showing your donkey the new arena, just as you would introduce him to anything new. Review the familiar turns on the haunches and forehand to build his confidence.

Attach drivelines to his bridle. With your assistant by his side with a lead rope, ground drive your donkey through an hourglass pattern. Be sure to use the usual verbal cues, "walk-on," "gee," "haw," and so on. Once he's made his way through the pattern, take him through the opposite way. Your assistant is only there for safety as you do the driving. The hourglass is a great pattern to solidify rein cues and voice commands, and it won't be long before your donkey is steering quite nicely and you can fade out the assistant!

When your donkey has mastered the pattern, take him to the rail and teach him to drive along it in a straight line. Your assistant may be necessary for this lesson; going straight isn't as easy as it sounds, and it is an important step in training.

Now try all of this with you in the saddle. Because you've only ridden your donkey in the roundpen, have your assistant ride ahead on an experienced animal. Your donkey should follow with minimal assistance. With your assistant in the lead for safety, go through the hourglass pattern. Make sure your rein and leg cues are gentle and consistent, and don't forget the rewards! When your donkey is going well, you can try it solo.

When he's secure with you on his back in the hourglass pattern, take him around the perimeter of the arena at a walk. Concentrate on keeping him straight, and make sure he responds to your command to "whoa" with a true stop. Again, fade out the assistant but keep her nearby for safety.

In the larger arena you are not interested in going any faster than a walk at this point in training. This is another instance where a donkey is different from a horse or mule. You are going to make sure he has absolutely mastered all the basics at the walk before you even think about trotting! Your goal now is to establish communication and control through the gentle use of the aids. Asking for or allowing a faster gait will confuse your donkey and create bad habits that might be difficult to overcome.

In fact, here's a trick if he ignores your command to whoa and tries to trot off. Stay calm, keep him straight, and "whoa" at the fence. Don't turn him! That's one of those bad habits he can develop. Keep him straight until he reaches the fence and understands that you want him to stop.

After a few lessons in the arena, take your donkey to the obstacle course. After all, you've been leading him through these obstacles, and so the next step should be easy. Take your time and have some fun ground driving him through them with an assistant.

It won't be long before you're both confident enough for you to drive him without the assistant.

Once he negotiates the obstacles smoothly, you can ride him through them. Again, your assistant should be at his head for safety but should be ready to back off if not needed.

In working your donkey on the obstacle course, you are perfecting your cues and his responses to them. This is an important phase of training, so don't rush—take several lessons and several days to make sure he masters each obstacle. It is in this practical application of the training that you will truly learn to appreciate his intelligence and his ability to learn!

To broaden the training routine and to keep both of you from getting bored, introduce some variety. Create an interesting schedule such as one day in the roundpen and the next in the open doing hourglass patterns. The third day might be on the obstacle course. Make sure each session includes a review of what he's learned, and ask for some flexibility exercises every time you mount.

Another reason you've kept your training to a walk is to allow you to learn how to communicate and negotiate with your donkey. You've probably noticed how smart he is, and how quickly he anticipates what you want. That's both good and bad, and you never want to get into a "Who's in charge here?" contest with your donkey. Reward the responses you want, but never try to bully your donkey—it simply won't work.

Prevent your donkey from anticipating and ignoring your cues by negotiating the obstacles in a different order each time. If he is reluctant to complete an obstacle, just go forward in a large circle, come back through the obstacle, but stop in the middle rather than at the end. Just this tiny modification will probably result in success. Negotiation! Give him every opportunity to succeed on his own. Use an assistant if needed.

Occasionally your donkey may resist your rein cues by sticking his nose out and pulling his head to the side. You can correct this problem by adjusting the elbow pull drawreins to an emergency drawrein position. Your goal is to prevent resistance. The emergency drawrein position is covered in detail in Videotape #4. (See also Appendix F.)

By now you've probably guessed another reason why we've done so much of your donkey's training under saddle at the walk: he has a tendency to freeze if he is frightened or confused. This is in direct contrast to a horse or mule whose instinct is to run!

Now you should determine if your donkey is ready for the next phase of training. Is he walking well in the roundpen while you lunge and ground drive him? In the arena, does he go through the hourglass patterns smoothly? Are his diagonals straight? Has he learned to respond to pressure by moving away? Are turns on the forehand and haunches becoming easier for him? The next step in training is to teach him to turn on the haunches while on the drivelines.

After he understands the turn on the haunches with the drivelines, try it with you mounted. Begin in the roundpen, then move to the open arena and practice along the rail.

Then go back to the drivelines to teach him the turn on the forehand. When you're ready to try this under saddle, remember to keep things slow and accurate.

If all is going smoothly, you are ready to speed things up a bit. If your donkey is willing to trot in the roundpen while tacked up, it's time to teach him to trot in the drivelines. Be patient—it won't be long until he's ready to trot with you on his back.

When he trots well in the roundpen, you can move to the arena for the familiar hourglass patterns. Adjust your drawreins from the elbow pull to the emergency drawrein position to help his balance at the trot and later the canter.

Adding the trot to the obstacle course takes planning and preparation on your part. Plan ahead for each obstacle. Trot to it first. Then come back and trot over it. Have an assistant nearby for help as needed.

If your donkey is having a bit of trouble with the hourglass pattern at a trot, have an assistant ride a trained animal through the movements while you follow a few strides behind. By seeing what you want, your donkey will quickly master trotting the pattern. Just be sure you don't ride too close to the animal in front.

Once he has mastered the hourglass, you may move to the perimeter of the arena. Walk the short side of the arena and trot the long sides. Soon you can add circles at various points. Always end training lessons with walk, halt, back.

Begin with a complete review in the roundpen: lunging at a walk and trot, ground driving at a walk and trot, and finally riding at the walk and trot.

When you've completed this warm-up review, dismount and go back to lunging. Ask your donkey to trot, then ask him to canter. Use the same sequence of commands you've always used—verbal first, then shuffle your feet while raising both arms, one holding the whip toward his rear and the other pointing the direction you want him to travel. Touch him above the hock and on the fence behind with the whip to reinforce your verbal command.

Even if he only canters a few strides, take this as a victory and ask him to "whoa." Reward him and do the exercise once more to make sure he understands. Then quit for the day.

Once he canters fairly well while lunging, you can mount him. Your assistant should stand in the center with the lunge whip to reinforce your cues. When he canters, sit quietly, with a loose rein, and allow him to lope until you say "whoa." After a few roundpen sessions he will be ready for the arena.

In the arena, it is a good idea to use an experienced animal to lead your donkey into a canter. Start with the familiar hourglass pattern at a walk and trot until he is settled.

Move to the perimeter of the arena and have the assistant begin to canter out of the short side and along the long side. This follow-the-leader game, combined with your verbal command to "canter," should encourage him to lope out! Don't worry about leads in these first few sessions—it's enough that he's cantering!

Once he has picked up the canter, let him lope as long as he likes, then reward him. Now each canter lesson should become a bit longer as you encourage him to maintain the pace. As he gains balance and strength, he will be able to sustain the canter longer.

Avoid letting your donkey trot faster when you ask him to canter. He should pick up the lope and maintain it. If he drops out of the canter to a fast trot, ask him to canter again immediately. If he still won't canter, just stop and begin again. You don't want him to develop any bad habits—you want him to know you are in control and he must do what you ask.

This is also a good time to add to his vocabulary of verbal cues, saying "canter-gee" as you track to the right and "canter-haw" as you track to the left. Use these cues as you canter around the perimeter, at each corner, and as you add large (50-foot diameter) circles.

Before long, you will be able to vary the patterns and refine your control by asking him to trot the short sides of the arena and canter the long sides.

You can also trot up the long side of the arena, do a turn on the haunches, and canter away on the correct lead.

You might shift the pace a bit by asking for more transitions from walk to trot or canter, and from canter to trot or walk.

As your donkey canters more and more, he will become better ing." Lateral movements will improve his balance, muscle strength, and flexibility. It's also the basis for any advanced training you might wish to undertake.

Now you can also pay closer attention to leads. Canter leads were covered in detail in Videotapes #5 and #6. It won't take long for your donkey to master the basics of cantering on the correct lead. You can start to really have some fun as your training reaches a new level!

When his transitions have improved and he has become better balanced, begin to canter smaller circles. To help him learn to take the correct lead, circle in the center and make changes of direction on the fence. He should be able to execute a quick turn on the haunches, coming out on the correct lead.

Watch in the video how I use circles and trot transitions to work my donkey into a simple lead change through a figure-eight. If he misses the lead in the center, you can use the fence to help bump him into the correct lead. If he misses a change of lead during any of these exercises, simply stop him and start the exercise again.

Donkeys are actually more responsive to verbal commands than to rein and leg cues, so don't forget to use verbal commands constantly. Be precise, be concise, but don't leave anything out!

Once your donkey is adept at the canter and changing leads with just a few trotting strides, you can teach him to change on a straight line.

Step 1: Begin at a walk, then trot, then canter-haw a small circle, then go straight for a few strides. Drop to trot, then canter-gee a small circle, straighten, and repeat on the straight line.
Step 2: Ask for the new lead without the circle. You may actually have to do a slight bend into the new circle, then go back to a straight line once he picks up the lead, but this should merely be an interim step.

Once your donkey has learned to canter and change leads in patterns and on the straight line, he is ready to begin "lateral training." Lateral movements will improve his balance, muscle strength, and flexibility. It's also the basis for any advanced training you might wish to undertake.

Chapter 1   Lateral Training

Lateral work begins with ground driving your donkey in a large arena. You may have an assistant at his head to help reinforce your cues and show him what's expected.

As always, review what your donkey has learned. Next, drive him through the familiar hourglass pattern, but this time, ask him to circle the first corner cone and proceed down the centerline as illustrated in the diagram in Appendix D. Here's where your assistant will help him begin to move forward and sideways away from the circle. The verbal command is "gee-over" or "haw-over." As he begins to move diagonally, so should you, step for step. Pull the outside rein with distinctive pulls and releases, pulling in unison with his front legs. Use your whip to tap his opposite hip. Yes, this takes practice and coordination, but soon you'll be moving as a team!

Once he's beginning to move laterally, you can add new patterns. You can also ask him to listen even more carefully to your rein and whip cues. Eventually you will ask for more complex patterns involving changes of lateral directions and moving his hindquarters. Appendix D shows details on these variations of the hourglass.

Sometimes you might want to teach these lateral lessons to your donkey while mounted, and then do the ground driving afterwards. This is where blunt spurs might be helpful. It's pretty much up to your donkey's style of learning and your preference—if it's easier to manipulate reins, legs, and a crop than it is drive lines and a whip, then saddle up! The principles are the same, and you must be just as clear with your verbal cues.

If you have ground driven with an assistant, you probably won't need one while riding. Reward your donkey lavishly for his honest attempts to do what you ask. Lateral movements are very taxing and it takes time to get the muscles in shape and flexible. If your donkey tires, he won't do the movements correctly. Or worse, he may pick up bad habits as he tries to avoid such effort.

Keep the lessons short and do lateral exercises only once or twice a week. Try to give him two or three days between lessons until he is properly conditioned.

One way or the other, your donkey should learn to drive and ride laterally. When he has mastered these skills in the arena, take him to the obstacle course and see how much fun it is to negotiate the course from his back. Your assistant can aid you in keeping your donkey's body straight and performing the movements correctly.

Up to now you have been schooling "leg yields." Leg yields are lateral moves on an angled track. You may also have worked a bit on sidepassing on the obstacle course. This is a lateral move straight sideways. Sidepassing is harder for a donkey than leg yields. Here are four exercises to help him perfect both leg yields and sidepasses. Again, blunt spurs will help reinforce your cues.

The first exercise is a spiral. Begin at the trot on a large circle and gradually spiral down to a smaller circle. When he is losing momentum, slow to a walk and spiral down to the smallest circle he is able to do. Keep him walking and begin to spiral back out, using your reins and legs to move him sideways back onto the larger circle. Use your crop at the shoulder and hip to encourage him to move sideways.

Do this several times until he understands what is expected. Then pick up the trot as the circle becomes larger, and leg yield at the trot to the largest circle. Each time he finishes the exercise, reward him.

When he's doing well at the walk and trot, ask him to canter a large circle while you begin to spiral down. At about halfway to the center of the circle, ask him to slow to a trot. Finish the spiral making as small a circle as he can manage at the trot. Then start spiraling back out to the larger circle. At the halfway point, pick up the canter and finish moving onto the large circle.

The next exercise is to leg yield your donkey along a fence line. Walk along the short side of the arena and as you move onto the long side, put him at a 45° angle. Use the reins and your legs to hold him in position as he leg yields the long side. Release and go straight as he comes back to the short side.

The third exercise is to leg yield him from the corner of the arena to the center of the hourglass pattern. Use the cones as guides.

The last exercise is to do the hourglass pattern but circle each cone gate. Appendix D shows these patterns in detail. Always walk the patterns first, and make sure your donkey is clear on what you want before attempting them at the trot. Take your time and do it right. Then reward his success. These exercises will improve your donkey's negotiation of lateral movements including the sidepass over the "T" poles.

Chapter 2   Lengthening the Stride

Once your donkey is at this stage of training, you might want to think of how to perfect his way of moving and put him in the proper frame. Helping him achieve the proper frame and good balance will not only improve his way of going, it will improve his appearance and make it easier for him to respond to your commands.

One way to help him learn to use his body correctly is by using the elbow pull. Here's how to adjust it properly. (See Videotape #2 for more detail regarding drawreins.)

The elbow pull helps keep his body in the proper position by not allowing his poll—his head—to raise much above the withers at all gaits and during turns or stops. It is reactive equipment—as long as he is going properly, it won't affect him. But as soon as he starts coming out of proper frame, it begins to work. The worse his error, the stronger the action of the elbow pull. It won't take long until he learns the most comfortable—and correct—position for him to carry his head and body.

Watch the video to see how the elbow pull helps during lateral movements. Watch how it also helps the donkey maintain his balance through transitions and changes of direction. The elbow pull was important throughout basic training, but it is even more important now that your donkey is carrying a rider. He must be encouraged to maintain correct posture through movements to avoid injury to himself from the added weight of a rider.

Now you can begin to work on lengthening your donkey's stride. You will do this in the big arena. With the elbow pull in place, trot the perimeter of the arena. Ask him to lengthen on the long diagonal from corner to corner. He should not merely trot faster; he should actually increase the distance between each step. As you approach the corner, shorten his stride and collect him up a bit.

Here's an exercise to help him understand what you want. Place four ground poles slightly to the left of center of the arena approximately 2.5 to 3.5 feet apart, depending on the size of your donkey. He should be able to step easily between them without touching them. Trot around the arena and over the poles. After he understands what you're doing, dismount and lengthen the distance between the poles by about an inch. Now trot him through them again. Each session, you can lengthen the distance between the poles, but do it only an inch at a time.

Posting the trot will help develop cadence, and before long you won't need the poles. Your donkey will lengthen his stride as he takes his cues from your body and legs.

Now you're ready to add a ground pole to the exercises at the canter to help you both learn to count and regulate the strides. Place one ground pole perpendicular to the long side of the arena. Canter the perimeter and as you approach the pole, begin counting out loud about three strides out. "One, two, three, pole." This will help you learn to gauge distance and measure your donkey's stride. It will also help your donkey learn to adjust his stride. You will notice that your donkey's canter becomes more balanced, rhythmic, and cadenced. Cross the canter pole several times from each direction, and before long your donkey will be more in tune with your aids. And don't forget to count out loud!

Chapter 3   Jumping

The next exercise is a wonderful way to condition your donkey, and if you plan to jump, it's absolutely essential. Set a cavelletti slightly to the right of center of your arena, with a ground rail one stride before and one stride after.

Begin on the rail at a trot, and as you approach the cavelletti, begin to count, "one, two, three, JUMP." After you have trotted over the cavelletti two times with ease, you may ask him to canter away to the rail and down the long side of the arena. Then take a break and a breather as a reward for his effort. Repeat the exercise—two trot approaches and one canter—three times one way with a breather, and three times the other way.

As he improves, you can eventually canter him to the cavelletti and away. Just remember to preface the canter with trot work.

All of these exercises help in conditioning and your donkey will become more agile, stronger, and better able to carry your weight. They help him learn balance and control, and assist in refining the connection between you and your donkey.

If you discover you have a jumping star, make sure you view Videotape #7 on jumping. You'll learn more about training, building jumps, and negotiating courses. We're seeing more and more mules in cross-county events and stadium jumping. Why not show everyone what your donkey can do!

The end result of all of your hard work is that you will have a donkey that is safe, obedient, and a pleasure to ride. And you've accomplished all this through RESISTANCE-FREE training! Aren't you proud of what you've done so far? When you're ready to do EVEN MORE with your donkey, view the videotapes on Intermediate and Advanced Saddle Training (Videotapes #5 and #6). You'll be ready for Bishop Mule Days or your own county fair in no time!

Throughout this tape we've talked about how training a donkey is similar to rearing a child. Both need our help to grow into reliable adults, with the simple investment of time and careful training. They must learn certain rules and behavior for things to go well. You, in turn, teach them with love, patience, understanding, and just the right amount of discipline. Your donkey will bond with you in this process, and in the end, you couldn't ask for a better friend and companion!

Have you ever had a massage? Remember how good it felt? An increasing number of people in the United States and abroad are recognizing that animals also benefit from massage. At the Lucky Three Ranch, we have found that therapeutic massage promotes relaxation and reduces stress. Massage stimulates healing after an injury, and provides significant relief from pain.

See Appendix I for more details about massage.

Your donkey may experience soreness when you ask him for some of the advanced moves discussed in this workbook. Massage can reduce muscle spasms. Greater joint flexibility and range of motion can be achieved through massage and stretching. All of this results in increased ease and efficiency of movement.

Other benefits include better circulation of both blood and the lymph system and deeper, easier breathing. All of these benefits lead to a healthier hair coat; faster healing time from injury or surgery; reduced pain, spasm, and swelling; reduced formation of scar tissue; and a strengthened immune system. We know that massage therapy works on people. Just wait till you see how well it works on your long-eared athlete!

APPENDIX A
More on Mule Health Management

HOOF CARE

Most mules should be trimmed every six to eight weeks. During some times of the year they can go longer between trims, but this depends on your climate and the condition of the ground in your area. The length of time your mule works each day and the health status of your mule are other considerations. Check with your farrier to determine how the conditions surrounding your mule or donkey affect his hooves. There are many different hoof dressings you can use depending on your climate conditions to help keep hooves healthy.

When a foal is one to two months old, consider trimming his feet. While the foal is growing, it is important for him to have his feet trimmed so that his bones and muscles will develop correctly.

Trimming and Shoeing

For most mules, moderate work on soft ground means that a trim every six to eight weeks is enough to keep the hooves healthy. There are times during the year when hooves grow slower and your animal may be able to go longer than eight weeks without a trim.

For most moderate athletics, regular "mule shoes" are just fine, but if you plan to compete seriously at the upper levels of horsemanship, it is advisable to determine what type of shoe would be best for your mule's activity. There are many different kinds of shoes such as "sliders" for the reining mules, "borium" for those who will be riding under slippery conditions, "racing plates" for the race mules, "tap and die" for cross-country mules—and the list goes on.

BASIC HEALTH CARE

Choosing A Farrier

The old saying "No foot, no mule" is literally true. When choosing a farrier, pick someone who is knowledgeable and experienced in his field. Mules are sensitive animals and respond best to people who are kind and gentle in their approach. It is important that your farrier has these qualities so working on your mule's hooves does not become a battle.

Choosing A Veterinarian

Mules get sick or have problems from time to time just like all of us. When they do, they need someone who is sympathetic and understanding of the way they feel. Choose a veterinarian who is kind, patient, and understanding in his or her approach as well as knowledgeable and experienced in veterinary medicine.

Your vet should be willing to discuss your mule's problem with you and help you gain more knowledge and understanding so that when help cannot arrive immediately, you have some knowledge of what to do until it gets there. This will help you and your mule feel more secure and happy.

Watching for signs of illness

The most obvious sign that a mule is sick is refusal to eat. The first thing to do if he is not eating is to take his temperature and check his gums to make sure they are still quite pink and not getting pale. Mules love to take "dust baths" and often this can be mistaken for colic. If your mule seems to be rolling a lot, you should stay and watch to see that he gets up and walks off and resumes eating. If he does, all is well. If he keeps rolling, grunts, and acts uncomfortable, there may be a problem. It's now time to call the vet.

Vaccinations

Shots are given based on your location. Consult your local veterinarian before proceeding. The main shots are usually given in the spring (March through April), one time, and then a booster is given in the fall (October through November). The 3-way and 4-way vaccines are pretty standard across the country, but there may be additional problems in your area such as rhinopneumonitus or Potomac horse fever. Be safe and consult your veterinarian.

Worming

Starting at birth, animals should be wormed regularly—about every eight weeks to keep their bodies healthy and parasite-free. If your mule is in a pasture with other animals, he will be at risk unless all the animals in that pasture have been wormed. One animal that has not been de-wormed can infect the entire pasture. The parasites are ingested through grazing. Worm medicines should be rotated to prevent the worms from becoming immune to the wormer. Check with your veterinarian for a viable and effective worming program.

Teeth

Check the foal's wolf teeth while he is still nursing. Wolf teeth are tiny canine teeth in the space in front of the molars. If they are not removed, they may interfere with the bit later and cause considerable pain for your animal and a resistance to training. Sometimes teeth can become sharp or get rough edges. It is important to check them and see if they should be floated. Again, consult your veterinarian.

Other body parts

Check your mule's ears for bug bites or any other kinds of irritations. Check his eyes for brightness and his nose for any discharge. His hair coat should be soft and shiny; dull coats can be the result of worms or other health problems. Look over his entire body and legs for any abnormal bumps or swelling. Check the hooves to make certain there is no hoof rot (thrush) starting anywhere. You will see soft blackish spots if the rot is setting in. Check your mule's manure to make sure it is neither too runny nor too hard. A change in the manure could mean a change in his health. Feeding time is a good time to take a few minutes to check your mule over each day, making sure he is happy and in good health.

Taking your mule's temperature

Temperature is one of the best indicators of animal health. Use a rectal thermometer designed especially for large animals. It should be large, stubby, quite thick, and less likely to break. Many are equipped with a string and alligator clip which can be clipped to the tail so it will not become lost if the animal swishes its tail and ejects it from the rectum. Thermometers should be stored in a cool place.

Begin by shaking down the thermometer to get the mercury toward the bulb end. Shake it all the way to the bottom for an accurate reading. It is helpful to use a lubricant such as petroleum jelly.

Stand at your mule's left hip, placing your hip against his so he will push you away if he moves. Grab the tail with your left hand while holding the thermometer in your right hand. Raise the tail slightly and insert the thermometer with your right hand, slowly and carefully until only about one-half inch is sticking out. Then clip the alligator clip to the top of his tail near his body. Leave the thermometer in place for three minutes. Remove it by removing the clip and grasping the string in your hand before taking it out. Pull it through a cleaning rag before reading.

The normal temperature for horses and mules is approximately 99.5° to 101.4° F (37.5° to 38.5° C). Foals and yearlings may have normal temperatures up to 102° F (39.0° C), especially if they are nervous or excited. Try to take repetitive temperatures at the same time of day to get accurate readings. Remember that in humid and hot weather, temperatures can be slightly elevated. A fever is not the problem; it's part of the healing mechanism. Your mule's survival may depend on how quickly you can find out why he has the fever!

Taking your mule's pulse

The pulse that you can feel in an artery is an intermittent wave caused by the heart forcing blood through it. The arteries alternate between expansion and contraction. It is this "pulse" that we feel and count. The easiest place to take the pulse is at the edge of the jawbone. Another place is behind the mule's left elbow. Or push the back of the hand firmly and flat against the chest wall. The heartbeat can be felt on the back of your hand. You can also learn to use a stethoscope to hear the heart rate.

An adult horse or mule should have a normal resting heart rate between 26 and 40 beats per minute. A foal two to four weeks old will have a heart rate of 70 to 90 beats per minute. The pulse of a foal six to twelve months old will be between 45 and 60 beats per minute, while that of two- and three-year-olds are usually around 40 to 50 beats per minute. The pulse rate increases in the evenings as compared to mornings. The pulse may be raised by hot weather, exercise, excitement, or alarm. It may be slower than normal with severe exhaustion, old age, or exposure to excessive cold.

Taking your mule's respiration

Respiration rate refers to the number of inhalations (or exhalations) per minute, the number of times the mule breathes in (or out). Don't count both in and out breaths or your respiration will be double of what it should be. Stand back and count the rise (or fall) or the rib cage. Do it from a distance with the animal standing quietly. If you have a stethoscope, you can use this if you are familiar with the different sounds you will hear.

Gut sounds

Gut sounds can be heard through a stethoscope. These are intestinal sounds, the tinklings and bubbling sounds made by gas as it percolates around and through the liquid and solid contents of the intestinal tract. By listening to both sides of your mule at the flank for several minutes you can get an idea of what is normal for him. No sound at all indicates a possible impaction or colic. You can also hear these sounds fairly well with your ear if you do not have a stethoscope.

COMMON MULE PROBLEMS

Mules are typically tougher and more durable than horses, but they can still suffer from many of the same equine problems. In most cases, the problems may be the same, but the mule has a less severe reaction than the horse. He still requires proper care.

Ear problems

The mule's ears are very large and open. Their only protection is the fine hairs within and without. In very cold weather, they can be susceptible to frostbite. Make sure your mule has shelter in inclement weather. The ears are also a favorite spot for warts to develop. Mites and parasites can find their way into your mule's ears fairly easily, so check often to make certain they look clean and healthy.

Mules who are brought up well usually do not have a problem with you handling their ears. If your mule suddenly does not want you to touch his ears, or if he tilts his head to one side, shakes his head frequently, or just doesn't seem to want you near his head, he may be having problems with his ears. Take the time to get to know what is normal behavior for your mule. Once you have done this, you will be better able to determine when he has a problem.

Bots

Bots are insects. They are flies that look like little bees buzzing around your mule. They lay small yellow eggs on the hairs and can be ingested by the mule. If he licks them, they can enter the digestive tract, hatch, and attach themselves to the stomach lining with their biting mouthparts. Another species of bots can attach to the terminal part of the rectum. If left unattended, they may eventually become so numerous that they perforate the stomach or lining of the digestive tract causing severe problems and possibly death.

One of the easiest ways to prevent infestation from bots is to remove the eggs from your mule's body hair daily with a bot knife or bot block. Rinsing with warm water will not remove the bots and will actually cause the larvae to hatch. A bot wormer is necessary to your worming program. Consult your veterinarian.

Hock sores

Though a mule is tough, he can be thin-skinned and sores develop easily in some areas of his body. The hocks are one of these areas. Sores on the hocks can turn into unsightly scars if left untreated. If your mule has these sores, it is probably due to lying on hard ground or in a stall with inadequate bedding. Consult your vet for a topical ointment.

Capped hocks and elbows

Capped hocks may be a blemish or an unsoundness. They may be caused by stall kicking, but this is hard to determine because you cannot always catch the animal in the act. An animal that kicks can teach this bad behavior to other animals. Capped hocks may be a conformation problem or lead to lameness, although in most instances they are merely blemishes.

Capped elbows are also called "shoe boils" because they most often occur when the mule hits his elbow with a shoe when lying down. They rarely cause lameness, but if they do, it is considered an unsoundness.

Abscesses

Abscesses are pockets of infection that can occur anywhere on your mule's body. If they are on the body, they are usually visible to the eye and can be drained by your veterinarian. If they are in the hoof, it is more difficult to pinpoint the exact location. If your mule has an abscess in the hoof, he will exhibit lameness and your veterinarian and farrier can determine the best course of action.

Colic

Colic attacks the digestive tract and can be mild or very severe and life-threatening. Some mules have a touch of colic several times a year. It is the equivalent of a stomach ache. In itself, it may not pose a problem, but if your mule rolls to alleviate his discomfort, he can twist an intestine and cause severe internal damage. Mules who are kept in dry lots or over-grazed pastures, are at risk for sand colic. They cannot help but ingest grains of sand with their feed that can do damage to the digestive tract. Your veterinarian can tell you what you should do in case of colic in your mule. Each case is different.

Founder and laminitis

Founder and laminitis are the names given to a foot problem in which the laminae in the hoof become inflamed. The laminae are delicate tissues and vessels which hold the hard shell of the hoof to the bone underneath. These can become inflamed from either infectious or non-infectious agents and the result is severe pain and lameness. In many cases founder is related to feeding problems. There are many different types of founder: grain founder, grass founder, water founder, road founder, and postpartum laminitis. It may also be related to hormonal problems. Though mules are less likely to founder than horses, they must still be monitored. The most obvious sign of founder is heat in the fetlocks, pasterns, and hooves of the front feet although it can affect all four feet. If you suspect founder or laminitis call your vet immediately!

Plant poisoning

Plant poisoning is an acute illness. It comes on rapidly and is often accompanied by violent symptoms such as frothing at the mouth and convulsions. Plant poisoning is hard to differentiate from some diseases such as Colitis-X. If you find your mule in trouble, check around to see if there is anything he might have eaten. If he is in convulsions, try to move him away from anything that might hurt him. Then call the vet immediately!

Ringworm

Ringworm is caused by a fungus that attacks the skin and lives in the hair follicles. It causes the hair shafts to become brittle and break. The damage spreads outward which results in circular marks on the skin and hair. The most common way that ringworm spreads is from mule to mule or horse to horse, although it can be contracted from other animals as well. Nutritional deficiencies will make an animal more likely to contract ringworm. Feeding a Vitamin A supplement throughout the winter can help.

Scours and diarrhea

Diarrhea in foals is called scours and is due to a bacterial infection. A foal can pick up the infection or he may simply have been weak and chilled the night of his birth. Foals generally go through a period of two to five days with scours, but this is easily treated with an anti-bacterial paste that you can buy in any feed store. If the problem persists, however, call your vet!

Diarrhea in any adult mule should be taken seriously. It could be the result of a simple feed problem, stress, or a bacterial infection such as Colitis-X. If your mule is off his feed, call the vet!

Tetanus

Tetanus is a bacteria commonly found in the equine's intestine and is passed through manure. It thrives in places where there is an absence of air. Tetanus can be a problem in humans from the same sort of punctures and wounds that cause it in mules or horses. Therefore, keep up to date on both you and your mule's tetanus vaccination.

Ticks

Mules infested with ticks will have a rough-coated appearance and may rub and scratch on fences and each other due to the irritation of the ticks. There are several species of ticks that attack equines in the mountain states. Though mules may not become as infested with them as a horses, they can still be affected and should be checked regularly if you have been in or live in an infected area. Ticks most often burrow under the jaw bone or between the hind legs. Treat them the same as you would lice.

Worm problems

There are several strains of worms that can affect your mule and if left unattended, they can even result in death. There is no way to isolate your equine from worms because he is a grazing animal, but worming every two months can minimize the risk. Consult your veterinarian about which drugs to use each time you worm.

Wounds

Wounds can range from the tiniest scratch to large gaping wounds and broken bones. Most wounds you will be able to dress yourself with topical ointments provided by your vet. Some wounds should be wrapped and others do better when they are left open to air. How you dress a wound will determine the amount of scarring you will see later. If a wound is deep, you should consider having it stitched. Consult your veterinarian to determine how best to treat your mule's wounds.

APPENDIX B
Unsoundness and Soundness in the Legs

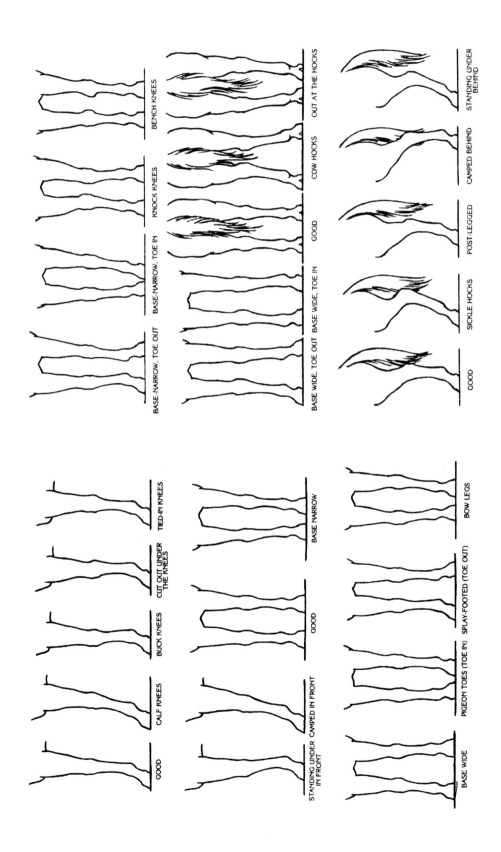

APPENDIX C
Showing At Halter (4-H)

Showing at Halter

Halter showing is an art and you, as an exhibitor, are in the arena to show your mule to the best advantage. Remember that the judge wants to see your mule, its conformation, soundness, and natural action. Have pride in your animal and your ability to show it. Learn to show your mule in a manner that will bring out its natural grace and beauty as it stands or moves.

Study the following points on halter showing. They are included in this appendix to remind you of what to do. Many will appear very simple, but show judges find they are not being practiced in many 4-H shows. Use them and you will become a better showperson.

General Points

Have the mule in condition and properly trained for show day. The hair coat should be smooth and glossy. The mule's skin should be loose and pliable with a clean, healthy appearance. The mule should show hard rippling muscles and its actions should indicate alertness and vigor.

Have the feet clean and trimmed; if shod, the shoes should fit and not show undue wear. The mane and tail should be trimmed or combed depending upon breed preferences.

Your equipment and personal dress should be neat and clean and should fit well. Use equipment and dress styles that will complement and not detract from the mule.

In the show ring: Be on time when the class is called. Enter the ring at a brisk walk and watch the ring steward for instructions on where to go.

Remember even though the ring officials may be checking entries, the judge may be sizing up the entries as they come in, so stay awake.

When instructed to line up, go around the line and enter from the rear in the position indicated. Line up evenly with the others and stand your mule. Try to get a position where your mule's front feet will be on slightly higher ground than the rear feet. Stand your mule quickly, then watch the judge.

Don't crowd the other mules. Allow room between your mule and those on either side. When the class is lined up head to tail don't crowd the mule in front—you may get kicked.

Posing: The mule should set-up quickly, stand squarely, and move forward or back freely. When using the safe areas, you are out of the direct line of a sudden lunge, a strike from the front legs, or a kick from a back leg. Because a mule uses its head and neck to balance its body, the safe areas are the positions where maximum control can be exerted by pulling the mule's head to the side. This forces the mule off balance, perhaps preventing further action if the mule becomes unruly.

Halter showing and showmanship customs today, especially in showmanship classes, encourage the showman to move to either side of the mule. This is safe if the mule is properly trained before entering the show ring. A mule acts independently on each side, therefore, you must train it to lead, stand, and show from each side. Experienced mule handlers will always handle a strange or untrained mule from the near (left) side because the majority of mules are started and handled from this side.

The shaded areas in the diagram indicate safe areas for showing a mule from either side. Note the danger zone directly in front of the mule. Learn to stand toward the front but out of the direct line of action of a strike or lunge. It is permissible to cross the danger zone to get from one side of the mule to the other. **Remaining in the danger zone is a fault.**

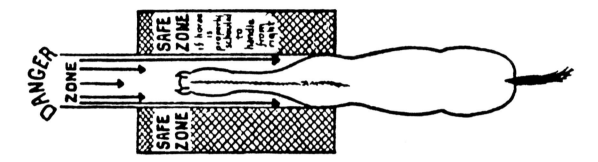

When lined up for a class, your mule should stand squarely on all four feet. You should remain in the safe zone on the near side and face slightly forward if the judge is working at the front of the class. If the judge is working at the rear of the class, you should turn and face to the rear (the lead strap may be switched to the left hand).

When necessary to let the judge inspect the near side, it's optional to step into the safe zone on the off side as shown in the drawing. You should not remain in the danger zone beyond the moment it takes to cross in front of the mule. A good showman will try to use positions within the safe zones where both the mule and judge can be observed. It is permissible for you to pass between the judge and the mule as the judge moves around the animal, but you should avoid blocking the judge's view beyond the moment required to step between the mule and judge. Step quickly and quietly.

The mule is trained to pose by use of the lead strap and soft voice commands. Kicking the legs into position is prohibited. Occasionally it may be necessary to touch the shoulder. The mule should move back and forward freely, executing a full step from just a slight shift of the weight. Always attempt to move the leg that is most out of position first. To change a back leg, move the body accordingly forward or back to shift weight, and touch the opposite shoulder. To change a foreleg, turn the head to the opposite side and shift the body accordingly. Turning the head slightly forces the weight onto the leg that is in position, freezing it in place, and frees the other leg for easy movement. You should train at home until the signals given are perfect.

Walk the mule in a straight line to the person standing at the other end. Move in a brisk, alert manner and allow enough slack in the lead rope for the mule's head to move freely. Stay to one side and don't block the judge's view of the mule's feet. When reaching the end of the line, stop a mule's length away from the person at this end. Wait for a signal to turn and go back. If this is where the judge is standing, he or she may wish to examine the mule so be ready to stand the mule squarely.

At the signal to turn and trot back, always turn to the right. This causes the mule to pivot in a collected, safe manner. Hold your right arm straight, gripping the lead strap close to the halter, and begin walking to the right around the mule. This will force the mule to turn the head and then the body within the circle you are walking.

Holding the mule back slightly will force it to pivot on its hind legs. A properly made turn will result in the mule standing squarely in its own tracks facing in the direction of the turn.

It may be necessary to make the mule take a step back halfway through the turn if it is not pivoting correctly on its hind feet. As the turn is completed, the mule will step forward to be in line. This is called the "Y" turn.

When the turn is completed, the mule is now facing the starting point. Hesitate just long enough to have the mule balanced, ready to move out. Don't stop and pose the mule, it should be trained to assume a square, balanced position immediately. Trot to the starting point.

Shallow turns may be made to the left when common sense applies but collection and control of the mule are important. The mule must be under control and not free to swing its hindquarters wide.

Leading: Lead from the left side of the mule with the lead shank held in your hand 8 to12 inches from the halter. Emphasis should be placed on light control of the mule with a minimum of pressure on the lead shank to allow the mule to hold its head naturally. A loose flopping lead strap is not acceptable. Excess strap is held loosely in the left hand in a figure-eight coil for safety.

The mule should move readily and freely at a walk or trot with a minimum of urging from you. You should stay in position at the near side of the mule's head and shoulder. A well trained mule will move readily at a speed equal to the speed at which you are moving. Three patterns are commonly used for showing the mule's way of going.

Show management should designate the pattern to be used, considering show ring space available and the judge's preference. Be familiar with all three patterns. The basic points of proper handling apply in all three patterns.

Pattern 1 — Lead the mule to the line indicated and stop a mule's length away from the person at the end of the line, facing in the direction you are to go. Hesitate just long enough to stand the mule squarely, ready to walk out in a balanced manner.

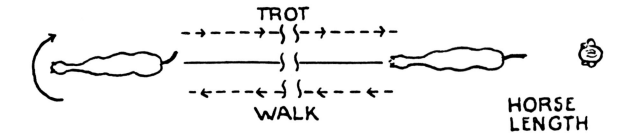

TROT

WALK

HORSE LENGTH

Pattern 2 — The class remains in line facing the judge as directed. Each exhibitor leads the mule at a walk toward the judge upon signal, halts a mule's length away, turns to the right upon the judge's signal, and trots away from the judge to the original position in line. The exhibitor should stop the mule and enter the line quietly. The ring steward should be alert to prevent accidents.

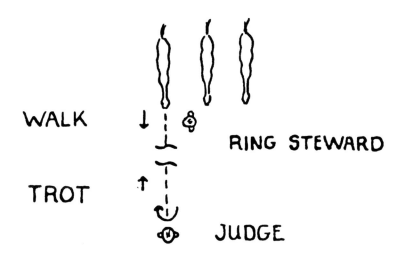

WALK

TROT

RING STEWARD

JUDGE

The judge then moves to a position opposite the next mule in line and indicates to the steward when he or she is ready. This is repeated to the end of the line.

Pattern 3 — The class is lined up head-to-tail at one side of the arena. Each mule is led to a point indicated by the ring steward, straight toward the judge. The exhibitor then turns and assumes a place at the end of the class line. The exhibitor should use care to travel in a straight line to and beyond the judge so the mule's action will be balanced and true.

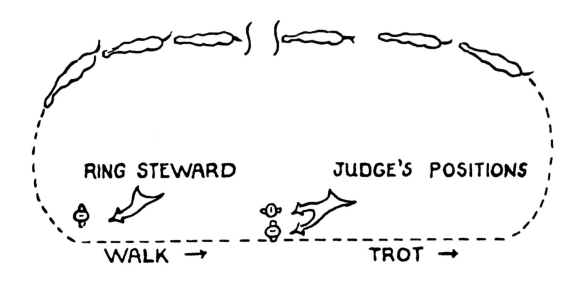

RING STEWARD

JUDGE'S POSITIONS

WALK →

TROT →

Ring Deportment

Showmanship is practiced from the time you enter the ring until you leave the ring. You should remain attentive for any instructions from the ring steward or judge. Be alert and watch other classes to know what the judge is asking other exhibitors to do. Your manners and actions reflect the time and effort you have spent in preparation and training.

Work calmly and quietly in the class. Keep the mule showing to its best advantage while you are in the ring. But remember, a mule cannot stand alert for the full time needed to judge most classes. Let your mule relax occasionally in position when you are certain the judge is not studying your end of the class. This does not mean letting your mule go to sleep or get out of line. Remember that people in the crowd will be watching you. Just let the mule shift weight and relax. You should watch the judge to be ready to prepare your mule for action.

While in the show ring your attitude should be businesslike, friendly, and cooperative and you should display a quiet confidence in your ability. Be a sportsman with other exhibitors. Dress in clothes that fit well and that reflect good taste. Expensive clothing is not necessary. Your hat should be in good condition and your boots should be shined. A tie and jacket are recommended if the weather is not too warm.

The placings have been made. Loser or winner, you are still being judged by the spectators. Retire from the arena in the same alert, brisk manner in which you entered. You want people to remember your mule as an alert, graceful animal. Your sportsmanship is showing!

APPENDIX D

Lateral Exercises on the Long Lines

Start with the basic hourglass pattern, excluding the circles. Add the circles after your animal becomes more proficient.

The following pattern is the **Hourglass pattern: Circling the Cones**

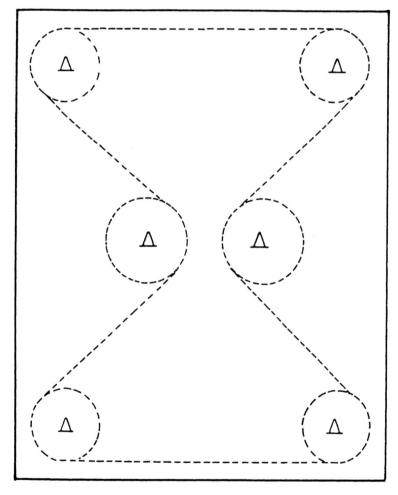

Circling the cones through the hourglass pattern helps the young mule to further collect his balance through turns. It will also increase his responsiveness to your aids.

APPENDIX D - Continued

Lateral Exercises on the Long Lines:

(A) Crossing the long diagonal

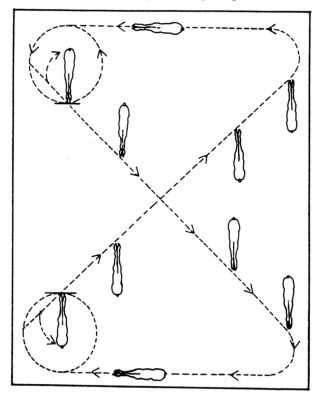

(B) Crossing the short diagonal

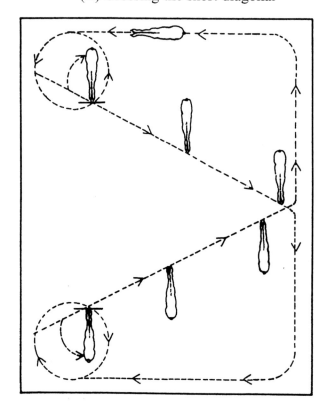

APPENDIX D - Continued

Lateral Exercises on the Long Lines:

(C) Change of direction through the center

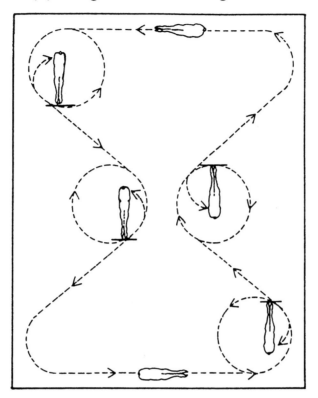

(D) Crossing two short diagonals

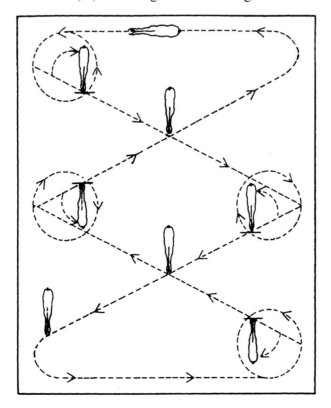

APPENDIX E
Obstacles

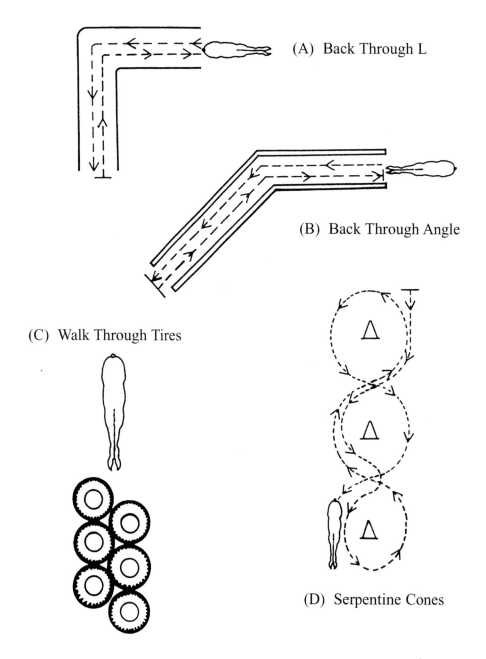

(A) Back Through L

(B) Back Through Angle

(C) Walk Through Tires

(D) Serpentine Cones

Obstacles

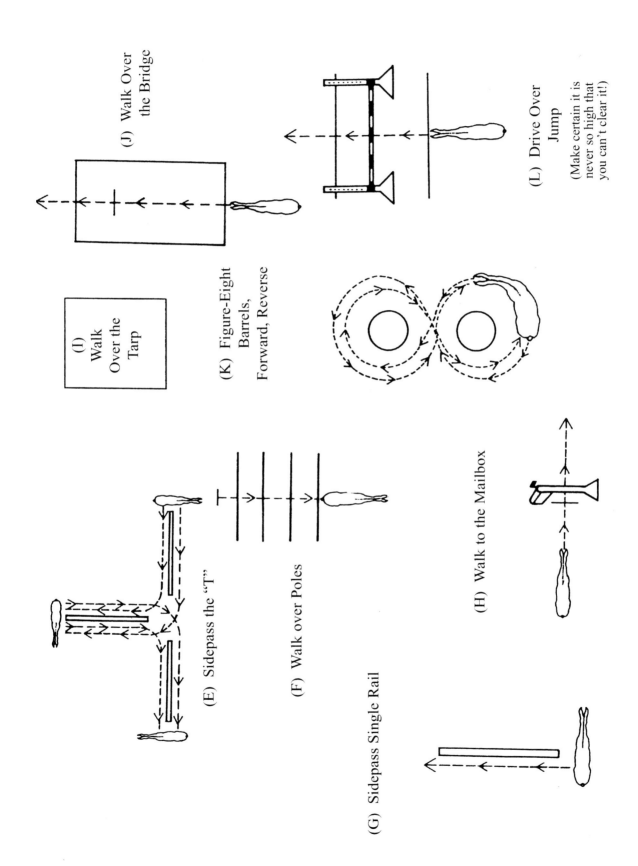

(J) Walk Over the Bridge

(L) Drive Over Jump

(Make certain it is never so high that you can't clear it!)

(I) Walk Over the Tarp

(K) Figure-Eight Barrels, Forward, Reverse

(E) Sidepass the "T"

(F) Walk over Poles

(H) Walk to the Mailbox

(G) Sidepass Single Rail

APPENDIX F
Drawrein Settings

Elbow pull drawreins: Use a 16-foot (5-meter) lightweight, soft cotton rope with snaps on each end. Fold the rope in half and drop it over the pole. Run the "reins" through the snaffle rings, then down between the front legs and up to the saddle.

Adjust the tension so that the poll is even or slightly higher than the withers. This puts pressure on the poll, the mouth, the elbows, and the back if your mule tries to raise his head too high. As long as he is in the proper frame, there will be no pressure.

Emergency drawreins: Use two lengths of rope, one for each "rein," with a snap on one end. Attach the snap ends high on the saddle (*left*) for the mule who carries his head too low; or attach them a little lower (*below*) for the mule that tends to carry his head too high.

APPENDIX G
Dressage Information

[The following pages are excerpts from The American Horse Shows Association Rule Book, 1997-98. Although the term, horse, is used throughout, you can apply the information to your mule or donkey.]

Object and General Principles

1) The object of Dressage is the harmonious development of the physique and ability of the horse. It makes the animal calm, supple, loose and flexible but also confident, attentive and keen, thus achieving perfect understanding with his rider.

2) These qualities are revealed by:
   a) The freedom and regularity of the paces;
   b) The harmony, lightness and ease of the movements;
   c) The lightness of the forehand and the engagement of the hindquarters, originating in a lively impulsion;
   d) The acceptance of the bridle with submissiveness throughout and without any tenseness or resistance.

3) The horse thus gives the impression of doing of his own accord what is required of him. Confident and attentive he submits generously to the control of his rider remaining absolutely straight in any movement on a straight line and bending accordingly when moving on curved lines.

4) His walk is regular, free and unconstrained. His trot is free, supple, regular, sustained and active. His quarters are never inactive or sluggish. They respond to the slightest indication of the rider, thereby give life and spirit to the rest of his body.

5) By virtue of a lively impulsion and the suppleness of his joints, free from the paralyzing effects of resistance, the horse obeys willingly and without hesitation and responds to the various aids calmly and with precision, displaying a natural and harmonious balance both physically and mentally.

6) In all his work even at the halt the horse must be on the bit. A horse is said to be on the bit when the neck is more or less raised and arched according to the stage of training and the extension or collection of the pace and he accepts the bridle with a light and soft contact and submissiveness throughout. The head should remain in a steady position as a rule slightly in front of the vertical with a supple poll as the highest point of the neck and no resistance should be offered to the rider.

7) The horse shows cadence when its movements are well marked, rhythmic and harmonious.

The Halt

1) At the halt the horse should stand attentive, motionless and straight with the weight evenly distributed over all four legs being by pairs abreast with each other. The neck should be raised, the poll high and the head slightly in front of the vertical. While remaining on the bit and maintaining a light and soft contact with the rider's hand, the horse may quietly chomp the bit and should be ready to move off at the slightest indication of the rider.

2) The halt is obtained by the displacement of the horse's weight on the quarters by a properly increased action of the seat and legs of the rider driving the horse toward a more and more restraining but allowing hand causing an almost instantaneous but not abrupt halt at a previously fixed place.

The Walk

1) The walk is a marching pace in which the footfalls of the horse's feet follow one another in "four time", well marked and maintained in all work at the walk.
2) When the four beats cease to be distinctly marked, even and regular the walk is disunited or broken.
3) It is at the pace of walk that the imperfections of Dressage are most evident. This is also the reason why a horse should not be asked to be on the bit at the early stages of his training. A too precipitous collection will not only spoil the collected walk but the medium and the extended walk as well.
4) The following walks are recognized: working walk, collected walk, medium walk, extended walk and free walk.

    4.1 **Working Walk.** A regular and unconstrained walk. The horse should walk energetically but calmly with even and determined steps with distinctly marked four equally spaced beats. The rider should maintain a light and steady contact with the horse's mouth.

    4.2 **Collected Walk.** The horse remaining on the bit moves resolutely forward with his neck raised and arched. The head approaches the vertical position, the light contact with the mouth being maintained. The hind legs are engaged with good hock action. The pace should remain marching and vigorous, the feet being placed in regular sequence. Each step covers less ground and is higher than at the medium walk because all the joints bend more markedly. The hind feet touch the ground behind or at most, in the footprints of, the forefeet. In order not to become hurried or irregular the collected walk is shorter than the medium walk, although showing greater activity.

    4.3 **Medium Walk.** A free, regular and unconstrained walk of moderate extension. The horse remaining on the bit walks energetically but calmly with even and determined steps, the hind feet touching the ground in front of the footprints of the forefeet. The rider maintains a light but steady contact with the mouth.

    4.4 **Extended Walk.** The horse covers as much ground as possible without haste and without losing the regularity of his steps, the hind feet touching the ground clearly in front of the footprints of the forefeet. The rider allows the horse to stretch out his head and neck without, however, losing contact with the mouth.

    4.5 **Free Walk.** The free walk is a pace of relaxation in which the horse is allowed complete freedom to lower and stretch out his head and neck. Free Walk on a Long Rein: Freedom to lower and stretch out his head and neck while still maintaining contact. Free Walk on a Loose Rein: Riding the buckle.

The Trot

1) The trot is a pace of "two time" on alternate diagonal legs (near left fore and right hind leg and vice versa) separated by a moment of suspension.
2) The trot, always with free, active and regular steps, should be moved into without hesitation.
3) The quality of the trot is judged by the general impression, the regularity and elasticity of the steps - originated from a supple back and well engaged hindquarters - and by the ability of maintaining the same rhythm and natural balance even after a transition from one trot to another.
4) The following trots are recognized: working trot, collected trot, medium trot and extended trot.

    4.1 **Collected Trot.** The horse remaining on the bit moves forward on the bit with his neck raised and arched. The hocks being well engaged maintain an energetic impulsion thus enabling the shoulders to move with greater ease in any direction. The horse's steps are shorter than in the other trots but he his lighter and more mobile.

4.2 **Working Trot.** This is a pace between the collected and the medium trot in which a horse not yet trained and ready for collected movements shows himself properly balanced and, remaining on the bit, goes forward with even, elastic steps and good hock action. The expression "good hock action" does not mean that collection is a required quality of Working trot. It only underlines the importance of an impulsion originated from the activity of the hindquarters.

4.3 **Medium Trot.** This is a pace between the working and the extended trot but more "round" than the latter. The horse goes forward with free and moderately extended steps and an obvious impulsion from the hindquarters. The rider allows the horse remaining on the bit to carry his head a little more in front of the vertical than at the collected and the working trot and allows him at the same time to lower his head and neck slightly. The steps should be as even as possible and the whole movement balanced and unconstrained.

4.4 **Extended Trot.** The horse covers as much ground as possible. Maintaining the same cadence he lengthens his steps to the utmost as a result of great impulsion from the hindquarters. The rider allows the horse remaining on the bit without leaning on it to lengthen his frame and to gain ground. The forefeet should touch the ground on the spot towards which they are pointing. The whole movement should be well balanced and the transition to collected trot should be smoothly executed by taking more weight on the hindquarters.

5) All trot work is executed sitting unless otherwise indicated in the test concerned.

The Canter

1) The canter is a pace of "three time", where at canter to the right, for instance, the footfalls follow one another as follows: left hind, left diagonal (simultaneously left fore and right hind), right fore, followed by a movement of suspension with all four feet in the air before the next stride begins.

2) The canter always with light, cadenced and regular strides, should be moved into without hesitation.

3) The quality of the canter is judged by the general impression, the regularity and lightness of the three time pace originated in the acceptance of the bridle with a supple poll and in the engagement of the hindquarters with an active hock action and by the ability of maintaining the same rhythm and a natural balance even after a transition from one canter to another. The horse should always remain straight on straight lines.

4) The following canters are recognized: working canter, collected canter, medium canter and extended canter.

4.1 **Collected Canter.** The horse remaining on the bit moves forward with his neck raised and arched. The collected canter is marked by the lightness of the forehand and the engagement of the hindquarters: i.e., is characterized by supple, free and mobile shoulders and very active quarters. The horse's strides are shorter than at the other canters but he is lighter and more mobile.

4.2 **Working Canter.** This is a pace between the collected and the medium canter in which a horse, not yet trained and ready for collected movements, shows himself properly balanced and remaining on the bit, goes forward with even, light and cadenced strides and good hock action. The expression "good hock action" does not mean that collection is a required quality of the working canter. It only underlines the importance of an impulsion originated from the activity of the hindquarters.

4.3 **Medium Canter**. This is a pace between the working and the extended canter. The horse goes forward with free, balanced and moderately extended strides and an obvious impulsion from the hindquarters. The rider allows the horse remaining on the bit to carry his head a little more in front of the vertical than at the collected and working canter and allows him at the same time to lower his head and neck slightly. The strides should be long and as even as possible and the whole movement balanced and unconstrained.

4.4 **Extended Canter.** The horse covers as much ground as possible. Maintaining the same rhythm he lengthens his strides to the utmost without losing any of his calmness and lightness as a result of great impulsion from the hindquarters. The rider allows the horse remaining on the bit without leaning on it to lower and extend his head and neck; the tip of his nose pointing more or less forward.

4.5 The cadence in the transitions from medium canter as well as from extended canter to collected canter should be maintained.

5) Counter-Canter ("False Canter"). This is a movement where the rider, for instance on a circle to the left, deliberately makes his horse canter with the right canter lead (with the right fore leading). The counter-canter is a suppling movement. The horse maintains his natural flexion at the poll to the outside of the circle, in other words, is bent to the side of the leading leg. His conformation does not permit his spine to be bent to the line of the circle. The rider avoiding any contortion causing contraction and disorder should especially endeavor to limit the deviation of the quarters to the outside of the circle and restrict his demands according to the degree of suppleness of the horse.

6) Change of Leg Through the Trot. This is a change of leg where the horse is brought back into the trot. After 2, or 3 steps, is restarted into a canter with the other leg leading.

7) Simple Change of Leg at Canter. This is a change of leg where the horse is brought back into the walk and, after at the most three steps, is restarted into a canter with the other leg leading with no steps at the trot.

8) Flying Change of Leg or Change of Leg in the Air. This change of leg is executed in close connection with the suspension which follows each stride of the canter. Flying changes of leg can also be executed in series, for instance, at every 4th, 3rd, 2nd or at every stride. The horse even in the series remains light, calm and straight with lively impulsion, maintaining the same rhythm and balance throughout the series concerned. In order not to restrict or restrain the lightness and fluency of the flying changes of leg in series, the degree of collection should be slightly less than at collected canter.

The Rein Back

1) The rein back is an equilateral, retrograde movement in which the feet are raised and set down almost simultaneously by diagonal pairs; each forefoot being raised and set down an instant before the diagonal hind foot so that on hard ground sometimes four separate beats are clearly audible. The feet should be well raised and the hind feet remain well in line.

2) At the preceding halt as well as during the rein back the horse, although standing motionless, moving backwards respectively, should remain on the bit, maintaining his desire to move forward.

3) Anticipation or precipitation of the movement, resistance to or evasion of the hand, deviation of the quarters from the straight line, spreading or inactive hind legs and dragging forefeet are serious faults.

4) If in a dressage test a trot or canter is required after a rein back the horse should move off immediately into this pace without a halt or an intermediate step.

The Transitions

1) The changes of pace and speed should be clearly shown at the prescribed marker; they should be quickly made yet must be smooth and not abrupt. The cadence of a pace should be maintained up to the moment when the pace is changed or the horse halts. The horse should remain light in hand, calm and maintain a correct position.

2) The same applies to transitions from one movement to another, for instance, from the passage to the piaffe and vice versa.

The Half-Halt

The half-halt is a hardly visible, almost simultaneous, coordinated action of the seat the legs and the hand of the rider, with the object of increasing the attention and balance of the horse before the execution of several movements or transitions to lesser and higher paces. In shifting slightly more weight onto the horse's quarters, the engagement of the hind legs and the balance on the haunches are facilitated for the benefit of the lightness of the forehand and the horse's balance as a whole.

The Changes of Direction

1) At changes of direction the horse should adjust the bend of his body to the curvature of the line he follows remaining supple and following the indications of the rider without any resistance or change of pace, rhythm or speed.

2) When changing direction at right angles, for instance when riding corners, the horse should be correctly bent and balanced, ridden as deeply as is appropriate to its level of training, into the corner.

3) When changing direction in form of counter-change of hand the rider changes direction by moving obliquely either to the quarter line or in the center line or to the opposite long side of the arena whence he returns on an oblique line to the line he was following when he started the movement.

4) At the counter-change of hand the rider should make his horse straight an instant before changing direction. When for instance at counter-change of hand at half-pass to either side of the center line the number of meters or strides to either side is prescribed in the test, it must be strictly observed and the movement be executed symmetrically.

APPENDIX H
First Level Tests

• Introduction to smaller circles

• Changes of bend

• Lengthening the trot

• Connection on the "long rein"

• Perfecting leg yields

• Lengthening the canter

• Riding the trot: sitting and rising

• Simple lead changes (change of rein through canter)

• Asking for more and less collection

• Serpentine in counter-canter (no change of lead)

FIRST LEVEL TEST 1

#		Test	Coefficient
1.	A X	Enter working trot Halt, Salute Proceed working trot	
2.	C E	Track left Half circle left 10m returning to the track at H	
3.	B	Half circle right 10m returning to the track at M	
4.	H-X-F F	Lengthen stride in trot rising Working trot sitting	
5.	A-C	Serpentine of 3 equal loops width of arena	2
6.	C	Medium walk	
7.	M-X-F F	Free walk Medium walk	2
8.	A	Working trot	
9.	K	Working canter right lead	
10.	E	Circle right 15m	
11.	M-X-K X	Change rein Working trot	
12.	F	Working canter left lead	
13.	B	Circle left 15m	
14.	H-X-F X	Change rein Working trot	
15.	A before A	Circle right 20m working trot rising. letting the horse gradually take the reins out of the hands Take up the reins proceed ahead working trot sitting	2
16.	K-X-M M	Lengthen stride in trot rising Working trot rising	
17.	E X G	Turn left Turn left Halt, Salute	

Leave arena at walk at A.

FIRST LEVEL TEST 2

#		Test	Coefficient
1.	A X	Enter working trot Halt, Salute Proceed working trot	
2.	C B E	Track right Turn right Turn left	
3.	A D-R	Down centerline Leg yield to the right (for small arena D-M)	
4.	C	Working canter left lead	
5.	E	Circle left 15m	
6.	F-M	Lengthen stride in canter	
7.	M	Working canter	
8.	H-X-F X	Change rein Working trot	
9.	K-X-M M	Lengthen stride in trot rising Working trot sitting	2
10.	C	Halt 5 seconds Proceed medium walk	
11.	H-X-F F	Free walk Medium walk	2
12.	A E B	Working trot Turn right Turn left	
13.	H-X-F F	Lengthen stride in trot rising Working trot sitting	
14.	A D-S	Down centerline Leg yield to the left (for small arena D-H)	2
15.	C	Working canter right lead	
16.	B	Circle right 15m	
17.	K-H	Lengthen stride in canter	
18.	H	Working canter	
19.	M-X-K X	Change rein Working trot	
20.	A X	Down centerline Halt, Salute	

Leave arena at walk at A.

FIRST LEVEL TEST 3

#		Test	Coefficient
1.	A X	Enter working trot Halt, Salute Proceed working trot	
2.	C E-X	Track left Half circle left 10m	
3.	X-B	Half circle right 10m	
4.	V-I I	Leg yield to right Straight ahead	2
5.	C M-X-K K	Track right Lengthen stride in trot rising Working trot sitting	
6.	P-I I	Leg yield to the left Straight ahead	2
7.	C H-X-F F	Track left Lengthen stride in trot sitting Working trot	
8.	A	Halt, 5 seconds Proceed medium walk	
9.	K-R R-M	Free walk Medium walk	2
10.	M C	Working trot Working canter left lead	
11.	S	Circle left 15m	
12.	S-K	Lengthen stride in canter	2
13.	K	Working canter	
14.	F-X-H	Change rein, at X change of lead through trot	
15.	R	Circle right 15m	
16.	R-F	Lengthen stride in canter	2
17.	F	Working canter	
18.	K-X-M	Change rein, at X change of lead through trot	
19.	C	Working trot	
20.	E	Circle left 20m trot rising. letting the horse gradually take the reins out of the hands	
before	E E	Gradually take up the reins Working trot sitting	2
21.	A X	Down centerline Halt, Salute	

Leave arena at walk at A.

FIRST LEVEL TEST 4

#		Test	Coefficient
1.	A X	Enter working trot Halt, Salute Proceed working trot	
2.	C M-X-K K	Track right Lengthen stride in trot sitting Working trot	2
3.	P B	Circle left 10m Turn left	
4.	E S	Turn right Circle right 10m	
5.	C	Halt 5 seconds Proceed medium walk	
6.	M-V V	Free walk Medium walk	2
7.	K A	Working trot Working canter in left lead	
8.	F-M	Lengthen stride in canter	2
9.	M	Working canter	
10.	C	Circle left 15m	
11.	H-X-K	Single loop with no change of lead	
12.	F-X-H M-F	Change rein, at X change of lead through trot	
13.	M-F	Lengthen stride in canter	2
14.	F	Working canter	
15.	A	Circle right 15m	
16.	K-X-H	Single loop with no change of lead	
17.	M-X-H	Change rein, at X change of lead through trot	
18.	A	Working trot	
19.	F-X-H H	Lengthen stride in trot sitting Working trot	2
20.	B X G	Turn right Turn right Halt, Salute	

Leave arena at walk at A.

APPENDIX I
Additional Massage Information

Massage for Donkeys and Other Equines

Has your equine ever had any of the following problems? Sensitivity to the girth? Restricted movement? Continual scuffing of the hind legs? Avoidance of leads? Problems bending? Lameness? Inability to lock the knees? Recurrent colic? Loss of power or coordination? Breeding difficulties when mounting or being mounted? Constant tail swishing? An uneven top line? Has he ever had surgery? Direct trauma? Resistance to training? Do you push him to the limit?

If you answered yes to any of these, your animal will benefit from massage. Massage is a non-invasive type of therapy that can address all of these problems and more when administered properly.

When we ride our animals daily and ask them for repeated movements such as in jumping, reining, or dressage, we put a lot of demand on the muscular and skeletal systems. This demand can shorten muscle fibers, restricting range of motion and putting undue stress on muscles and joints. Unforeseen problems can result such as lameness, arthritis, disk degeneration, or worse—a ruptured disk. These crippling disfunctions do not always wait for the animal to age before they appear.

Simple massage can prevent various injuries throughout your animal's lifetime. Don't wait for obvious injury to occur. Preventive massage increases the length of the muscle fibers, taking pressure off the joints. When the muscles are allowed to contract and expand to their full length, they are able to absorb important nutrients that reduce fatigue. Massage also increases blood flow which helps the body flush harmful toxins, such as lactic acid, that build up from normal use. Massage aids in reprogramming the nervous system to break patterns that can cause atrophy or knotted tissue.

The following information is an introduction to some of the basic techniques of massage that will enable you to identify areas of discomfort in your equine. It is not intended to replace the care of a licensed massage therapist or veterinarian. If you are unsure as to the severity of an injury, consult your vet!

Palpate along the neck beginning behind the ears and working your way back to the shoulder. Make sure to check the entire neck from poll to shoulder. Is one side more sensitive than the other?

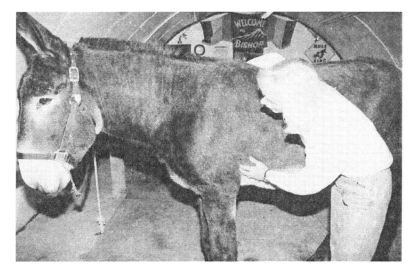

Ribs are a very sensitive area. Check each rib and between the ribs. If your donkey is nippy while being cinched, or refuses to change leads, it could be from soreness in this area.

As you massage your equine, keep in mind how massage should feel. Keep the pressure light over bony areas like the ribs, back, and poll. Heavily muscled areas such as the neck and hips can endure more pressure. Always be aware of your animal's reaction to pressure and respond appropriately. Watch his eyes and ears. Look for signs of sensitivity such as biting toward the affected area as you work, raising and lowering the head, moving into or away from pressure, contraction of muscles from your pressure, throwing the head, swishing the tail, picking up his feet, changes in breathing, or wrinkles around the mouth. If there is sensitivity in the neck, the shoulders and upper back may also be involved. If there is soreness in the hips, the ribs and lower back may be involved.

The neck is a good place to begin your massage. Make small circles with your fingertips. Imagine them as eyes, searching out lumps and bumps under the skin that are knots in the muscle fibers. Start behind the ears and work your way back to the shoulders. If your animal is heavy in the bridle, if he tips his head to one side, or if he has difficulty bending through the neck, he is exhibiting stiffness in this area.

Next massage the shoulders and between the front legs. Compare the two sides of the chest muscles. Is one side larger than the other? The shoulders work as shock absorbers and need the strength to pick up the front quarters when jumping. If there is soreness in these areas, your animal will have difficulty performing some athletic movements.

Ribs are a very sensitive area and can refer pain in many directions. Make sure to check each rib and the area in between them. Keep in mind that they span from the back to the belly; this is a large area of sensitivity due to the lack of muscle cover. Include the back when working on the ribs. Use your fingertips to feel each vertebra and compare each side for symmetry. If you keep this area relaxed and flexible, your equine will bend more easily through his body.

Because muscling is thick in the hip area, you might want to use a fist to exert more pressure there. Knead the muscles as if you were kneading dough. The animal will push into your hand to let you know that it feels good. If he moves away, he is telling you that you are exerting more pressure than he can endure comfortably, and you should go back to using your fingertips. When massaging the hips, the lower back and last few ribs should be included. Soreness in this area can result from jumping, collection, sliding stops, and rollbacks, for example.

Passive range of motion exercises involve moving limbs and joints as they were naturally intended to move. They should be gentle and easy. If you encounter resistance, just stop and try again. Forcing motion can cause tearing of the muscles and a breakdown of the trust you are trying to achieve. In order to do passive range of motion exercises, your animal must be able to trust and "let go," allowing you to manipulate the limb without resistance. If you have an animal that resists, do only as much as he will allow. Over time, he may loosen up and allow you more control. If he doesn't let go, don't force the movements; it will foster more harm than good. Some animals are just intolerant.

When moving the limbs and joints, be sure to stay within your animal's comfort zone. Be aware of the point where your animal begins to resist and stay behind that point. As your equine begins to trust and understand, and as his muscles and joints loosen, he will afford you a wider range of motion.

A raising of the head and perking of ears may indicate sensitivity. He is asking for lighter pressure. Learn to pay attention to the things your animal tells you about his body.

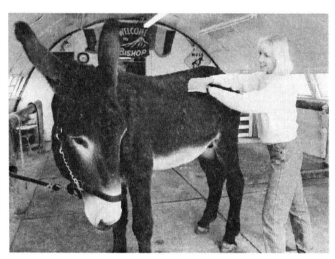

This animal is still concerned about the pressure. Sometimes you will feel your pressure is so light it can do nothing, but less is best.

Now he is happy with the pressure. He has dropped his head and has taken a deep breath. If you are doing rollbacks, sliding stops, or collection, this area can be very sensitive.

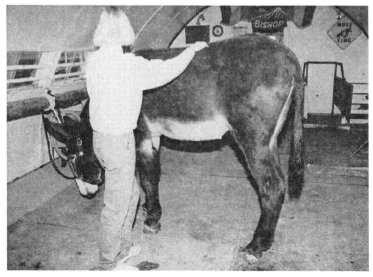

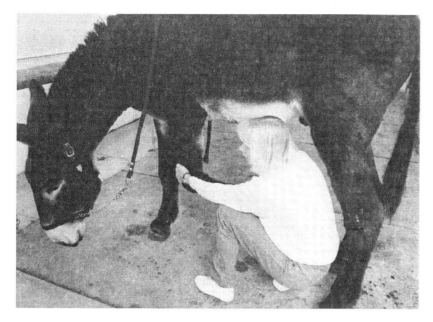

The front legs are a good place to begin your passive range of motion exercises. Be prepared to let go and get out of your animal's way. Shake the limb under the animal, then move the limb forward and back. Be aware of his limitations. Each time you work with him his range will increase.

Small circles are another technique for passive range of motion. The movement reprograms the nervous system and builds trust between you and your animal.

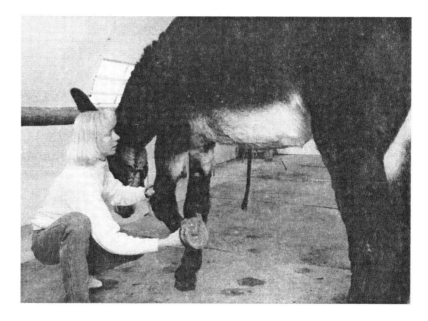

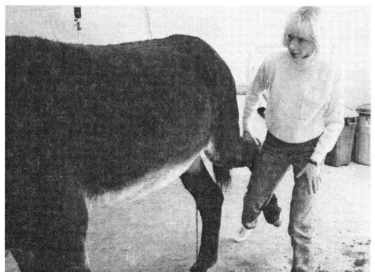

This is an advanced movement and will take some practice and time to achieve the desired result. Passive range of motion should be done within the animal's tolerance. Time will increase his degree of tolerance.

Massage therapy should never be harmful! For the sake of safety and comfort, do not attempt massage therapy for rashes, boils, open wounds, severe pain, high fevers, cancers, blood clots, severe rheumatoid arthritis, swollen glands, broken bones, direct trauma, or if there is any chance of spreading a lymph or circulatory disease such as blood poisoning. Avoid direct pressure on the trachea.

Massage therapy and passive range of motion exercises are good to do after a ride. It is easiest to find sore spots and muscles when your animal is warmed up. This is also the best time because you will aid the body in ridding itself of toxins that build up in muscle tissues and eventually cause stiffness. You do not need to massage your entire animal every time you work. For example, if he is having difficulty with leads, you may just want to massage the ribs and mid-back. Each time you ride, take the time to quickly go over your animal and assess his sensitive areas; check his range of motion to detect stiffness in the joints. Paying this kind of attention to his body will enhance his athletic performance and provide a wonderfully relaxing reward!

This movement is wonderful to make sure that the girth is not pinching after he is saddled.

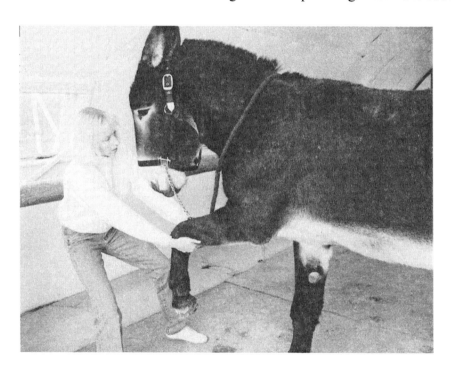

GLOSSARY OF TERMS

Aids: The means by which the rider communicates with his animal. There are two types of aids. Natural aids include the voice, legs, hands, and seat. Artificial aids include the bit, reins, whip, and drawreins.

Appointment: Show hobbles are an appointment and are sometimes attached to the saddle in Western show classes. They are considered dangerous to use on an animal.

"Back": Four-beat gait in reverse; also used as a verbal command.

Bank: A jump from one ground level to another.

Bi-directional: Jumps that can be jumped both directions.

Bit: Tack equipment that is placed in animal's mouth, providing a source for communication between animal and rider.

1. **Curb bit**—a bit with shanks and a chin strap or chain; indirect rein.
2. **Snaffle bit**—allows rider to use "direct rein" most efficiently. It does not have any shanks and works directly from the corners of the mouth. It can be solid or jointed.

> **Full-cheek snaffle**—a smooth, jointed bit with cheek pieces on either side of the mouthpiece to keep it from being pulled through the mouth.
>
> **Eggbutt snaffle**—a smooth, jointed bit with egg-shaped rings hinged to the mouthpiece such that it won't pinch the corners of the mouth.

Borium shoes: Any of several variations of shoes with beads of borium welded on at strategic points to prevent slipping.

Breast collar: Wide strap that wraps around the chest of the mule and attaches to the saddle or harness on both sides. It is usually held up by a narrower strap that attaches to both sides of the chest piece and runs over the mule's neck just in front of the withers, preventing the saddle from slipping backwards.

Breeching: Rigging draped around the rump, usually attached to a saddle or harness surcingle for the purpose of facilitating backing, going down a hill, or holding a pack in place.

Bridle: Headgear used for riding or driving.

Burro: Spanish word for small donkey.

By or sired by: Refers to the male parent of a horse.

"Canter": Three-beat gait slower than a gallop, faster than a trot. One of the animal's natural gaits. The canter has three beats followed by a moment of suspension. For a canter on the right lead, the sequence of legs is: left hind, one beat; right hind and left fore simultaneously, second beat; right fore, third beat. Also used as the verbal command.

Canter pole: Rail placed on the ground used to count strides to a jump.

Catch rope: Working rope or lariat.

Cavalletti: A set of ground rails attached to X-stands at either end such that they can be rolled into position at three different heights.

Change of rein: Change of direction. The rider can change rein diagonally across the ring, straight across the center, or through the circle.

Circles: Should be truly round and of a predetermined size when training. For example, a large circle is 20 meters or 60 feet in diameter. Start with large circles and decrease in size as animal gains strength and balance.

Collection: Back is rounded in a convex arc from head to tail; the stride is shortened, hocks are driven well under the body, and the action is more elevated, slower, and more animated. The tempo of the gait remains the same but the animal covers less ground; he lifts his legs higher and takes shorter, lighter, more cadenced steps. It is characterized by energy, the feeling that the animal's lowered hindquarters are a coiled spring ready to expand (see also Extension).

Colt: A male horse under three years of age.

Combined training: Dressage, stadium, and cross-country jumping combined.

"Come": Command for mule to come to you, either on the flat or over obstacles.

Conformation: The build of a horse, donkey, or mule; the structure, form, and symmetrical arrangements of parts.

Cross country: Course (usually measured in miles or kilometers) with multiple jumps along the way.

Cross-rail: A jump with standards where only one end of the rails is held on each standard so that the rails form an "X" in the middle.

Crupper: Strap attached to the saddle and looped over the tail to keep the saddle from sliding forward.

Cups (jump): Convex metal pieces that attach to the standard and hold the rails in place.

Direct rein: Act of guiding the animal to go left by pulling on the left rein and right by pulling on right rein.

Donkey: The domestic ass.

Dressage: Exercises and training of the horse to respond to subtle aids and develop muscles evenly with correct posture.

Egg bars: Shoes shaped in a continuous oval with no break at the frog; they provide more support than regular shoes.

Elbow pull: Used as a training aid. Can be made from a 16-foot (5-meter), lightweight, soft cotton rope with a snap on each end. It is one of many positions for drawreins.

English saddle: Lightweight saddle with no horn, limited fenders (flaps), and stirrup irons.

Equitation: The art of riding horseback; horsemanship.

Extension: Lengthens the animal's frame and stride so that he goes forward with increased impulsion and a lowered head and neck. The tempo of the gait remains the same but the animal covers more ground with increased suspension (see also Collection).

Face tie: Tying a mule's head to a fence so he cannot turn into you.

Farrier: A horseshoer.

Fenders: Western term for the part of the saddle directly under the rider's legs above the stirrups; called "flaps" in English terminology.

Figure-eights: Two connecting circles.

Filly: A young female horse under three years of age.

Flash noseband: Noseband that attaches to a regular cavesson and is strapped around the nose in front of the snaffle bit.

Flat-withered: Flat over the shoulders.

Foal: A baby equine under six months of age; a young, unweaned horse of either sex.

Forehand: The animal's front legs, head, neck, shoulders, and withers.

Frame: Correct posture for any given stage of training.

Free lunging: Basic commands for free lunging are walk, trot, canter, whoa, and reverse. No tack except the halter is used while free lunging.

Full seat: When the rider is sitting with full weight in the saddle and in full contact with his legs and seat; balanced seat.

Gait: A particular way of going, either natural or acquired, characterized by a distinctive rhythmic movement of feet and legs. The animal has three natural gaits—walk, trot, and canter. All three gaits are required at all levels of dressage competition in varying degrees of collection and extension, such as working, collected, medium, and extended trots.

Gallop: Three-beat running gait of an equine.

"Gee": Verbal command used for turning right.

Gelding: An altered or castrated horse.

Girth: Folded leather or webbing held with girth straps on English saddles to keep the saddle in place. On Western saddles it is called a "cinch."

Girth straps: Straps attached to the saddle for holding the girth in place. Latigo is the term for a Western strap.

Ground driving: Directing your mule with rein cues while walking behind him.

Ground line: Invisible line on the ground, parallel to the first rail of fence or parallel to the first part of the jump you encounter.

Ground poles: Poles (usually four total) spaced on the ground to affect your mule's gaits; also called "rails."

Gymkhana: Equine games such as barrel racing, pole bending, and so on.

Gymnastics: Series of jumps designed as aerobic exercise for equines.

Hackamore: A type of Western headstall or bridle without a bit.

Half-chaps: Chaps of leather that cover the lower leg of a rider.

Half-halt: A barely visible, almost simultaneous, coordinated action of the seat, the legs, and the hands of the rider, with the object of increasing the attention and balance of the horse before the execution of movements or transitions.

Halter: Head gear used for general ground management of an equine.

Hand: The unit by which the height of an equine is measured. A hand is equal to four inches.

"Haw": Verbal command used for turning left.

Headstall: The part of the bridle that encircles the equine's head and holds the bit. It includes the crown piece, brow band, cheek pieces, and noseband.

Hindquarters: The animal's hind legs, rump, and croup.

Hinny: Hybrid cross between a male horse (a stallion) and a female donkey (a jennet).

Hobbles: Restraint used to control an animal.
1. **Scotch hobble**—immobilizes the hind legs safely, one at a time.
2. **Sheepskin-lined chain hobbles**—two fleece-lined cuffs attached together with a chain.

Horse mule, john mule: Male mule.

Imprinting: The act of touching your animal all over his body, including orifices such as the mouth and ears, to accustom him to your touch, your voice, your smell, the way you look, and the way you interact with him.

Impulsion: A thrusting action originating from the hindquarters that is a result of engagement of the hind legs under the body. The animal steps forward and under with his hind legs. Impulsion adds energy, brilliance, and keenness to the animal's movements.

Indirect rein: Procedure for guiding the animal usually using a curb bit; neck rein.

Inside: The side away from the rail, or toward the center of any curve or circle. The rider's inside leg is the leg on the inward side of the ring. In lateral movements, inside refers to the side toward which the animal is bent.

Jack: Male donkey.

Jennet, jenny: Female donkey.

Jog: Two-beat, very slow trot.

John mule: Male mule.

Kimberwick: Bit commonly used for cross country with a mild curb action and chin chain, but it maintains use of a direct rein.

Lateral bend: The animal's spine is bent to the curve of a circle.

Lateral moves: Sideways or angled movements; any deviation from the straight line.

Lead line: Lead rope; any line that is attached to the halter and used to encourage the animal along.

Lead shank: Lead line or rope with a section of chain on the end nearest the mule.

Lope: Three-beat, very slow canter.

Lunge line: Line used for circling the mule around you, 20 to 25 feet (6 to 8 meters) in length.

Lunge whip: A whip long enough to reach an animal on the lunge line or in the roundpen

Lunging: Circling your animal around you either on a line or in a roundpen.

Mare: A mature female horse three years or older.

Molly mule: Female mule.

Mule: Hybrid cross between a male donkey (a jack) and a female horse (a mare).

Near side: The horse's or mule's left side.

Neck strap: Strap used around the mule's neck for the rider to grab for balance.

Negative reinforcement: A negative reward for a behavior; punishment.

Non-slip reins: Reins made with grips to prevent slipping through the hands.

Novice: Combined Training Division in which jumps are between 2'6" and 2'11" high.

Off side or far side: The horse's or mule's right side.

On the flat, flatwork: Any equine activities not involving jumping or leaping.

Out of, dam of: Refers to the female parent of an equine.

Outside: The side closest to the rail or to the outside of any curve or circle. The rider's outside leg is the leg that is next to the rail. In lateral movements, outside refers to the side opposite the bend of the animal.

"Over": Verbal command used for lateral moves.

Oxer: A jump with two or more elements having a slope and a spread.

Packsaddle: Saddle with a frame to hold panniers or "packs."

Pastern: The section of bone between the fetlock joint and the hoof.

Poll: Area between the ears.

Positive reinforcement: A positive reward for a behavior; a treat.

Pre-Novice, Beginner Novice: Combined Training Division in which jumps are between 2'3" and 2'9" high.

Reins: Control straps of varying lengths depending on use.

Resistance: When the animal lets the rider or handler know he would rather not do what is asked of him by grinding his teeth, wringing his tail, hollowing his back, sticking his nose in the air or tucking it into his chest, pulling on the rider's hands, getting the tongue over the bit, freezing, or running off.

"Reverse": Command to change direction.

Romal: A long flexible quirt or whip attached to closed reins.

Roundpen: Round corral, usually 45 to 55 feet (14 to 17 meters) in diameter.

Sacking out: Gently placing the saddle blanket or other frightening obstacle on an animal's back, sliding it from head to tail, slowly and calmly. This is to help the animal become accustomed to the saddle and other tack. Also used to desensitize his body.

Saddle blanket: Tack placed between the saddle and the animal's back for comfort and stability.

Safety release bars: Devices for holding stirrup leathers in place on English saddles and sidesaddles.

Seat: The rider's physical position in the saddle. A dressage rider needs a balanced seat: he should be sitting straight in the deepest part of the saddle, erect but relaxed, allowing himself to follow the movements of the animal and able to use his aids without changing the position of the rest of his body.

Serpentines: Evenly spaced "snaky" patterns; a series of loops or half-circles all the same size, used to teach the horse lateral bending. Serpentines help develop and supple both sides of the animal equally.

Show jumping: Usually associated with breed shows; done in an arena with consideration to faults and speed.

Showmanship: The activity surrounding showing your equine to others from the ground in a halter.

Side reins: Lunging reins connected from bit to girth rings with some degree of "stretch" to them. They do not "slide" as drawreins do.

Snaffle rings: Rings attached to the bit on both ends.

Sound: A term meaning the horse is physically fit and shows no signs of weakness or illness.

Splint boots: Protective coverings for the legs.

Stadium jumping: Jumping done in a confined area, usually as an element of combined training, with consideration to faults.

Stallion: Mature male horse used for breeding.

Standards: The 4" x 4" self-standing posts drilled with holes every three inches (1 cm) for holding jump cups.

Straight: One of the fundamental rules of dressage is "straighten your animal and ride him forward." He is straight when his backbone is parallel to the track he is on and his hind feet follow the track of his forefeet without deviating to the side.

Surcingle: Strap with D-rings on it that fastens around the animal's girth for lunging.

Suspension: The moment in the trot or canter when the animal has all four feet off the ground.

Tack: Riding equipment or gear for the equine, such as saddle, bridle, and halter.

Tap and die shoes: Shoes made with holes drilled in them for "cleats" to prevent slipping.

Tempo: Frequency of footfalls. The tempo of a given gait does not change when going from collection to extension; the number of times the animal's feet hit the ground per minute remains the same. Often used interchangeably with rhythm.

Three-point: When the rider is sitting with lightened weight in the saddle, with legs in full contact with the animal, and with his seat lightly touching the cantle while most of his weight is borne in the stirrups. The position may vary but the center of balance should be maintained.

Transition: Any change of gait, or movement, or lengthening of stride. Transitions must be smooth and quickly and quietly done, but not hurried.

"Trot": Two-beat forward gait, faster than a walk. Also used as a verbal command.

Two-point: When the rider is standing in the stirrups in a crouched position with legs in full contact with the animal. The position may vary but the center of balance should be maintained.

Type: The ideal representation embodying all of a breed's characteristics.

Vertical: Jump that is constructed straight up and down.

Volte: A circle.

Walking the course: Examining a course to determine the best path to follow, best line to a jump, how many strides between jumps, and the safest way to negotiate them.

"Walk On": Four-beat gait forward, slowly. Also used as a verbal command.

Weanling: A young equine under one year of age who is no longer nursing (weaned from mother).

Western saddle: Heavy saddle with large fenders, skirts, and a "horn" on the front.

"Whoa": Command used for stop.

Wings: Rails placed on either side or both sides of a jump to channel the mule to the center and over.

Withers: Top of the shoulders at the base of the neck.

Wolf teeth: Tiny canine teeth in the space in front of the molars.

Yearling: An equine who is between one and two years of age.

INDEX

See also the **Glossary of Terms** on pages 115-119

Videotape Series / Book Order Form

Date: _____

Order Made by:
Name _____
Address _____
City _____
State _____ Zip _____
Country _____
Phone # _____
Fax # _____
E-mail address _____

Ship to (indicate if different):
Name _____
Address _____
City _____
State _____ Zip _____
Country _____
Phone # _____
Fax # _____
E-mail address _____

Where did you see our products? _____
Have you ordered from us before? _____ If yes, when & what products? _____

Description	Qnty	Price	Sub Tl
Tape #1: Foal Training		$ 39.95	
Tape #2: Preparing for Performance: Ground Work		39.95	
Tape #3: Preparing for Performance: Driving		39.95	
Tape #4: Basic Foundation for Saddle		39.95	
Tape #5: Intermediate Saddle Training		39.95	
Tape #6: Advanced Saddle Training		39.95	
Tape #7: Jumping		39.95	
Tape #8: Management, Fitting and Grooming		39.95	
Tape #9: Keys to Training the Donkey: Intro to the Donkey		39.95	
Tape #10: Keys to Training the Donkey: Saddle Training and Jumping		39.95	
Autographed hardbound book *Training Mules & Donkeys: A Logical Approach to Longears* (222 pages)		39.95	
Condensed Workbook of Tapes 1 - 7 *Training Without Resistance: Foal to Advanced Levels* (220 pages spiral bound book)		19.95	
Condensed Workbook of Tapes 8 - 10 *Equine Management and Donkey Training* (128 pages spiral bound book)		19.95	
Hardbound book *Donkey Training* (157 pages)		39.95	
Minus any DISCOUNTS			
SUB TOTALS			
** SHIPPING/HANDLING	—	—	
SALES TAX (if Colorado resident add 3%)	—	—	
TOTAL DUE	—	—	

** See Tables for costs for Shipping/Handling <u>INSIDE</u> the U.S. & <u>OUTSIDE</u> the U.S.

Payment Method: Amount Paid $ _____

☐ VISA   ☐ Mastercard   ☐ Check (check #_____)   ☐ Money Order _____
☐ Discover   ☐ American Express

Cr Cd # _____ Exp. Date_____Signature_____

Shipping and Handling Charges

Shipping <u>within</u> the United States:

Method	Ground Service	Priority Service
Delivery Time:	7 - 14 bus. days	3 - 7 bus. days
If your order total is:	**Your shipping and handling charge is:**	
0 - $50.	$ 5.00	$ 12.00
$ 50.01 - $100.	$ 10.00	$ 16.00
$100.01 - $200.	$ 15.00	$ 22.00
$200.01 - $300.	$ 20.00	$ 30.00
Over $300.01	**Call for Rates**	

Shipping <u>outside</u> the United States:

MethodGround	Service	Priority International Mail
Delivery Time:	25 - 30 bus. days	14 business days
If your order total is:	**Your shipping and handling charge is:**	
0 - $50.	$ 9.00	$ 28.00
$ 50.01 - $100.	$ 13.00	$ 31.00
$100.01 - $200.	$ 18.00	$ 36.00
$200.01 - $300.	$ 22.00	$ 55.00
Over $300.01	**Call for Rates**	

THIS COUPON GOOD FOR
$5.00 off

Your next purchase of <u>one</u> of Meredith Hodges' videotapes

Send this coupon with your purchase. You may send more
than one coupon if you are making a multiple title order.
One coupon per videotape title. The video title must be
different in order to receive the discount.

Example: If you are ordering 5 videotapes,
(one of Tape #1, one of Tape #2, one of Tape #3, one of Tape #4, one of Tape #5),
you can send in 5 coupons for a $5.00 discount on each tape --
or a total of $25.00 savings [5 tapes multiplied by $5.00]

This offer is not good with any other discounts or wholesale pricing.

Training Mules and Donkeys
A Logical Approach to Longears

Videotape and Book Series Titles

Tape	Tape Title	Description of Contents
Tape #1	Foal Training	• What are the differences between horses, mules, and donkeys • Neo-natal isoerythrolysis information • Understanding your foal • How to handle, tying techniques, leading, showmanship, and trailer loading
Tape #2	Preparing for Performance: Ground Work	• Lunging in a roundpen • Ground driving • Restraints and breaking bad habits • Bitting
Tape #3	Preparing for Performance: Driving	• Pre-hitch training • Fitting the harness • Carts and carriages • Hitching to the vehicle • Reinsmanship • Pleasure driving • Obstacle driving and pulls
Tape #4	Basic Foundation for Saddle	• Mounting • Riding in roundpen • Riding in open • Riding over obstacles • Grooming and care of hooves
Tape #5	Intermediate Saddle Training	• Equitation • Lateral work • Collection • English/Western Pleasure • Advanced obstacles/trail
Tape #6	Advanced Saddle Training	• Equitation • Dressage • Western Riding • Reining • Preliminary jumping
Tape #7	Jumping	• Equitation over fences • Ground poles • Cavalletti • Verticals • Oxers • Gymnastics • Courses

Tape #8	Management, Fitting and Grooming	• Housing • Feed • Nutrition • Health care • Braiding • Showmanship • Bathing, vacuuming, clipping
Tape #9	Keys to Training the Donkey: Introduction and Basic Training	• Differences between the donkey and mule • Imprinting for foal and adult • Tying and leading • Obstacle course • Trailer loading • Showmanship • Measuring for athletic potential • The donkey jack
Tape #10	Keys to Training the Donkey: Saddle Training and Jumping	• Basics in the roundpen • Trotting • Mounting • Patterns and obstacles at the walk and trot • Cantering • Advanced training • Lateral training • Lengthening the stride • Massage for your athlete
BOOK	*Training Mules and Donkeys: A Logical Approach to Longears*	222 pages hardbound book. A no-resistance training manual. Ask for an autographed copy. Price: $39.95 + $5.00 s/h
BOOK	*Training Without Resistance: From Foal to Advanced Levels*	220 pages spiral bound workbook consisting of information from Videotapes 1 through 7, plus MORE! Price: $19.95 + $5.00 s/h *We have translated this book into Spanish, German and French.*
BOOK	*Equine Management and Donkey Training*	128 pages spiral bound workbook consisting of information from Videotapes 8 through 10, plus MORE! Price: $19.95 + $5.00 s/h *We have translated this book into Spanish, German and French.*
BOOK	*Donkey Training*	157 pages hardbound book. Details differences in training donkeys. Price: $39.95 + $5.00 s/h

For Ordering Information

Call: 800-816-7566 or 970-224-5911
Fax: 970-472-0753
Write: MediaTech Productions
         P.O. Box 272345
         Fort Collins, CO 80527
Customer Service and Orders: 1-800-816-7566
Website: www.mediatechproductions. com
Email: maury@mediatechproductions.com
Payment: VISA, MC, Discover, Am. Express,
             check, Money Order
European Market: We have PAL conversion videos

Questions? Or for more info?

Write: Lucky Three Ranch, Inc.
         c/o Meredith Hodges
         2457 S. County Road 19
         Loveland, CO 80537
Call: 970-663-0066
Fax: 970-663-0676
Email: lucky3@willman.com
Web Page: www.LuckyThreeRanch.com

Retailers!   **Ask about our dealer prices**
Customers!   **Ask about our discount if you purchase seven or more tapes.**
                 You will receive a $20.00 discount on your seventh videotape.